WHAT THEY DON'T TEACH YOU ABOUT INDIAN MANAGEMENT STYLE

Unveiling R.O.S.H.I.N.I - the *Bharatiya* way of managing

Anand Kumar R.S.

INDIA • SINGAPORE • MALAYSIA

ISBN 979-8-89277-948-7

Dedicated to

All those who read my weekly blogs and liked,
commented, critiqued and shared, which gave me
the confidence to write a book.

Contents

Foreword..7

Chapter 1   Introduction 11

Chapter 2   Japanese Style of Management.................... 15

Chapter 3   American Style of Management.................... 29

Chapter 4   Indian Style of Management 42

Chapter 4A   History of Management in India.................... 43

Chapter 4B   Diversity of Management Styles in India................ 52

Chapter 5   Exploring the Aspects of the Indian
Style of Management.................... 67

Chapter 5A   Business is a Family.................... 68

Chapter 5B   In Relationships, We Trust 73

Chapter 5C   Business is for the Long Term 78

Chapter 5D   Not Sticking to the Knitting 81

Chapter 5E   Flexible Indians.................... 87

Chapter 5F   Thriving in a Crisis 94

Chapter 5G   Family Owned, Professionally Managed................ 101

Chapter 5H   Indians and Decision Making.................... 106

Chapter 5I   Indian Businesses and Ethics 113

Chapter 5J   Innovation in Indian Companies 119

Chapter 5K   India – The Land of Jugaad 126

Chapter 5L   Indian Marketing 131

Chapter 5M   The Indian Manager 140

Chapter 6   Conclusion 147

References 151

Acknowledgements 155

Foreword

Back to the Future Part 1: Peek into the 1990s and land into any B school campus during placements. You will see Multi-National Corporations hogging Day 0 and Day 1 and except for a few Indian companies, others will be lucky to get into Day 2 and Day 3.

Back to the Future Part 2: Present day - Indian companies across Industry segments are the preferred destinations for B School students.

This massive transformation has many fathers.

Obviously, the 1st wave of economic *Perestroika* of 1991 laid the foundation. However, one of the critical changes was the rapid professionalisation of the Indian companies personally led by the founders. The next-gen in these transformed companies also grabbed the baton with alacrity and set them on a blistering growth path catalysed by booming domestic consumption and investment-led growth.

The stable political climate over the last decade also has emboldened the scions to look at massive investments in India and abroad, transforming Indian companies into true transnational companies. Indian companies have also invested in the best practices in HR and ensured focus on talent acquisition, retention and management. Many of these Indian companies regularly feature in the list of the best companies to work in India.

Traits like having a loyal team around you and even having a clan bias which were viewed with disdain are being grudgingly accepted as strategies that do work in some circumstances! The result is today, we have many Indian companies that dot the global skyline as "Great" companies.

It is in this context that this work by Anand Kumar on the Indian Management style gains significance.

But who is Anand and why am I writing about him?

Back to the Future Part 3 – Circa 1970s!

Ancient civilizations have predominantly thrived and prospered on the banks of great rivers. Throw in a fertile and busy mind in that alluvial soil and you get a picture of Anand growing up at Trichy, a historical town drained by the river Kaveri.

Anand was my schoolmate in Trichy and our friendship went beyond professional and other distractions and has stood the test of time.

Anand's leadership was amply in evidence right from our school days. He was an integral part of our school's English plays. All of us were voracious readers of English and Tamil literature and the town's limited libraries could not offer enough fodder to our appetite. Reading and discussing endlessly about what we read was our favourite pastime in a TV or internet-free era!

We lost touch for a decade and his name cropped up during my management traineeship days from a colleague who was an MBA batchmate of Anand. I was not surprised to hear Anand's insightful and entrenched innings at the MBA school. We did connect after 20 years and Anand was just like where we left off in 5th class – on the go always. He had blossomed into a seasoned management professional, but at the same time did lots of writing on varied subjects - from Current affairs to Marketing to Politics to Movies to Slice of life.

It is this civilisational upbringing in a busy town formalised by Engineering and Business education and his passion for writing that has made Anand do the natural progression of sharing his thoughts on the Indian Management style on which a lot of material is not readily available, in the form of a book. Read on and Lead on!

Gopalakrishnan P
Chennai
March 2024.

Gopalakrishnan is currently the Managing Director for India, Middle East and South East Asia markets for a US based Organization. An alumnus of the College of Engineering, Guindy and IIM Kolkata, Gopal has over 30 years of corporate experience spread across India & Southeast Asia regions in diversified domains. He is an avid weather watcher and his interests are as varied as Nature, Weather Cricket, Movies and Travel.

Chapter 1

Introduction

"Most of what we call management consists of making it difficult for people to get their work done."

- Peter Drucker

The year was 1990. India had not yet liberalised its economy and was still an inward-looking country in all aspects. I was in the first year of my MBA programme. Gurcharan Das, author, management Guru, and public intellectual, was heading Procter and Gamble (P&G) in India as its first CEO then. On an invitation from our institute, he came to deliver a guest lecture in which he talked about P&G's strategy in India and how their products, like Whisper, became market leaders despite being more expensive than those of their competitors like Carefree. He also spoke about Ariel, their detergent powder brand in the same length. In the Q&A session that followed, Das answered a wide range of questions from a youthful audience that was in awe of him and his success in the corporate world. One question from that session I remember vividly was if there was something called the Indian management style. He replied that an Indian style probably exists but will get talked about when more and more Indian companies succeed globally as the American and Japanese companies did. This thought stayed with me, and in the past three decades, I have constantly been checking if the time has come to characterise the Indian management style.

In the 90s, homegrown groups like Tata, Birla, Reliance, RPG, and others dominated the Indian corporate space. But their operations were by and large limited to India, and they didn't have a footprint outside of India or had a limited presence outside. Today, three decades later, the landscape is totally different. The economic reforms of 1991 opened up the Indian economy to global competition like never before, removed protectionism with which the Indian companies were thriving till then, and sowed the seeds for the rapid economic growth in India, which we have been witnessing since the dawn of this century. The reforms also unleashed the animal spirits of the Indian private sector, which was hitherto protected from global competition. Even then, the last two decades firmly belonged to China, which clocked a consistent 10%+ growth for years together and firmly got into the league of big economies. Today, its economy has slowed down, yet at US$17 trillion, it is the second largest economy in the world, just behind the United States of America.

In terms of growth rate however, China is no longer the fastest-growing economy globally, a tag that China owned for over a decade. Today, among the large economies, India has emerged as the fastest-growing and, in size, has overtaken the United Kingdom this year. At this point, there is a global consensus among commentators that the next few decades will be India's. Naturally, compared to 1990, when Indian companies had just local ambitions, today, many Indian groups have become transnational corporations with a global footprint.

Indian company names are no longer new to people outside India. An iconic brand like *Land Rover* is owned by the Tata Group. A company like Infosys is considered an icon in the software industry and is among India's first global success stories. An automotive ancillary manufacturer like Bharat Forge[1] is among the leading engine and chassis components suppliers to international customers. It enjoys a strong relationship with over 36 global customers and is identified as a strong long-term supply partner by leading worldwide OEM and tier-1 customers.

India, or for that matter, Indians and Indian companies, are no longer seen patronisingly or with the kind of disdain today by the world outside as probably they were, a few decades ago. Professionals from India are now accorded respect for being technology and management experts. The Indian Institute of Technology (IIT) is a brand that has a broader brand recall in the United States than most things from India. Therefore, it is not a surprise that today, more than ten global tech giants, including Google (Alphabet) and Microsoft, are headed by Indians. It is not just the tech companies; even a consumer product company like Pepsi was headed by a person of Indian origin - Indra Nooyi until 2018. In 2014, she was ranked number 13 in the Forbes World's 100 Most Powerful Women and was ranked the second most powerful woman on the Fortune list in 2015 and 2017. Last year, another consumer retail giant, Starbucks, named an Indian-born Laxman Narasimhan their global CEO. I believe this trend will only strengthen further in the future, and we will see many more Indians occupying the coveted corner rooms in global corporations.

At the same time, three decades ago, it was unimaginable to see a foreigner as a CEO of an Indian company. But today, many Indian companies are headed by foreigners working out of India. We also now see many foreigners, even from developed countries like the United States and Australia, coming to India and working in Indian companies. These days it is common to see many foreigners being hired by Indian companies in their units abroad. This also points to the emergence of Indian companies as entities to reckon with in the global corporate arena. Cometh the success cometh the recognition.

Back to the question posed to Das and his answer, I believe that the time has now come to define and spread the concept of the

Indian style of management. As India becomes one of the largest economies in the world, which it is poised to, there will be keener interest in India as a country. There will be an increased quest worldwide to understand its people, culture, and way of doing business. This book aims to focus on the business part, particularly the Indian way of management and its essential traits.

In the coming chapters, we will examine the history of business in India and the background of the Indian management style. As in most things in India, an important question that needs to be answered is - Can one homogeneous style emerge for the entire country in a diverse country like India? To answer this, we first look at the distinct business styles available in India itself and then boil down to some of the typical traits of the Indian style of management. Also, before we talk about the Indian style, it is essential to quickly analyse the other globally established styles, like the American and the Japanese styles, to appreciate the commonalities and divergences, if any, compared to the Indian style.

Chapter 2

Japanese Style of Management

"Japanese management practices succeed simply because they are good management practices."

– Masaaki Imai, Japanese Management Guru

I worked in a large Japanese group for more than ten years, and before that, I had the opportunity to interact with Japanese companies and Japanese people for another five years. I also had the chance to visit Japan over a dozen times, almost all on business. Working in a Japanese company, interacting with Japanese people, and visiting the country often helped me observe and build my own idea of the Japanese management style apart from reading about it. Source material on the Japanese management style is available in plenty, and it is not difficult to fathom the reason. In the post-World War II global order, the success of Japan and it becoming an economic powerhouse while being such a small country is a story with very few parallels. Therefore, the world looked at Japan and hypothesised how Japan succeeded as an industrial nation.

Japanese products, from cars to appliances, started flooding global markets, mainly developed countries like the US and Western Europe first and then developing countries. As a small country, Japan realised that exporting its products to other countries was the only way to succeed. This also meant that the products had to meet global quality standards; therefore, the Japanese companies focused on product quality first. Japanese brands like Toyota,

Sony, and Honda, to name a few, became household names because of their superior quality. "Made in Japan" attracted a premium everywhere. Further study of how the Japanese could manufacture high-quality products consistent across product categories led the world to study and understand the Japanese manufacturing system. Toyota, the car manufacturer, adopted the Japanese manufacturing system, which came to be known as the Toyota Production System (TPS).

The Japanese Manufacturing Techniques:

Some of the concepts from the Japanese manufacturing system that became popular globally include JIT (Just in Time), *Kaizen, Kanban, Poka-yoke*[2], *and Ishikawa*[3] (Fish Bone diagram). Many of these techniques have found resonance in manufacturing industries worldwide since the late '70s. Various books and papers started getting published on these that made the Japanese manufacturing system the toast of the town. "The Study of the Toyota Production System from an Industrial Engineering Perspective", a book authored by Shigeo Shingo, an engineering consultant in 1989, is a popular academic material on the Japanese manufacturing system in general and the Toyota Production System in particular.

Since enough reference material is available on the various aspects of the Japanese manufacturing system, I am not getting into details of it. All these concepts originated from a production or shop floor perspective but were soon applied in other management functions as well. So, even a sales or service department soon adopted *Kaizen* or continuous improvement.

To a large extent, aspects of the Japanese management style derive from the critical elements of the Japanese manufacturing system. Having observed the functioning of Japanese companies from close quarters, in my opinion, the Japanese management style revolves around the following:

1. Thinking in the Long Term:

Decision making is based on a strategic and long-term view rather than a short-term tunnel view. Short-term loss to gain a long-term advantage is considered acceptable. For example, Japanese companies do not shy away from investing in R&D for core technology development, which may take years to yield results. Similarly, most Japanese companies do not believe in burning capital and spending on disproportionate advertising and marketing expenses to gain short-term market share. Instead, they would prefer to build the brand gradually with limited marketing spending while keeping a close watch on the company's bottom line. Clearly, the thinking is that companies must serve the stakeholders and society at large for many generations to come and not just be there to make money that quarter. It is rare to find a Japanese company exiting the business very soon based on a few quarters' losses as they believe in long-term success, and so they are prepared to take any short-term slide in their stride. This aspect of the Japanese has been researched and confirmed in many behavioural studies.

2. Conservatism in Budgeting and Rigour in meeting it:

In most Japanese companies, the budget prepared at the beginning of the year is everything. Once the budget is finalised, it is cast in stone. The same is broken down monthly, quarterly, and across the organisation. Then afterwards, periodic reviews still happen against the budget, and the budget is expected to be achieved. Even if market conditions change dramatically in the year, the original budget is not revised, and a review still happens based on that.

Since the whole organisation focuses on achieving the budget, conservatism is at the heart of the budgeting exercise. At the same time, the expectation is that budgets are meant to be achieved. There is no expectation to over-achieve, and it is perfectly all right to slow down once the budgets are achieved in a year.

Talking of conservatism, the other aspect of the Japanese is to do everything step-by-step instead of going the whole hog. For instance, instead of launching a product country-wide, most Japanese companies would launch first in one market, make it a success, introduce it in three markets, and then go for a national launch. This also ties into their risk-averse nature, which will be covered separately later.

3. Flexibility is a Disease:

Whether it is product planning or sales, Japanese companies do not believe in keeping things flexible. Masaaki Imai is a Japanese organisational theorist and management consultant best known for his work on *Kaizen*. One of his famous quotes stresses the importance of standardisation and shunning variety and flexibility. *"Where there is no standard, there can be no improvement. For these reasons, standards are the basis for maintenance and improvement."*

Flexibility is considered a recipe for uncertainty and confusion within the organisation. Therefore, whether it is the number of SKUs (Stock Keeping Units) for sales production forecasting or go-to-market plans, a Japanese company would like to keep things firm and work towards the same, even if this means losing business opportunities in the short term. For example, there could be large bids or government tenders for products in which the order size will be far higher than the monthly average sales. Deciding to participate in the bid would mean being flexible regarding factory lead time, as the customer would not place firm orders in advance and would require goods with shorter lead times. While an American or Korean company would be flexible in its lead time for such large bids, a Japanese company would prefer to skip the bid rather than take a chance of building inventory or being flexible in its lead time to fulfil the order.

The Japanese strongly believe that being flexible is a disease and therefore they always stick to their time schedules. Meetings start on the dot and finish on the dot as per schedule. There is no question of extending them even if an issue is still open.

4. Risk Mitigation is Critical:

In my experience, Japanese companies have low or no risk appetite. Therefore, risk mitigation is the cornerstone of their decision making. There is a widespread perception, which is also largely accurate, that Japanese companies are extremely slow in decision making, and this general aversion to risk is the main reason. Concluding a commercial agreement with a Japanese company and getting down to business quickly can be an arduous task. They take a lot of time to go through each and every clause of the agreement, its short-term and long-term impact, and risk analysis. When a business case is presented, they look at it from all angles, even if it means several buses are missed. On the other hand, the aversion to risk keeps Japanese companies financially stable and strong.

You will see that most Japanese companies do not conduct business on open credit. The payment terms will be either 100% in advance or need to be backed by a letter of credit or bank guarantee, etc. Even in cases where they decide to operate on open credit, it will be only after availing of credit insurance. So, they don't believe in conducting business without secured collaterals. We all know that "credit" is a business enabler. Not offering credit, therefore, has a dampening effect on sales and can be a spoiler. Yet, Japanese companies would rather bear the loss of sales than endure receivables that entail risk.

Talking about risk aversion, many Japanese companies mandate that staff use an anti-glare shield for company laptops so that it is not easy to figure out what they are doing when working in public spaces. And exchanging data on pen drives with outsiders is, of course, a strict no-no.

While the above are examples of the risk-averse nature of the Japanese at the micro level, it becomes dense and deep at the macro level. Let me cite an example. Japanese banks like the Bank of Tokyo Mitsubishi or Sumitomo Mitsui Bank operate primarily with just one branch in India. I believe that the primary purpose of these banks is to protect the financial interests of their Japanese clients doing business in India. So, when a Japanese company sets up a subsidiary in India, it is more likely that the capital gets routed through the Japanese bank only. From here, on a need basis, money is transferred to another Indian bank, which has a more country-wide retail presence for day-to-day operations. This is a classic example to explain the risk-averse attribute of the Japanese. So, they believe that even if something happens to the Indian bank, their capital is safe being parked in a Japanese bank account.

Foreign companies that conduct business in Japan will tell you how complex it is to carry out banking transactions in Japan because many Japanese companies only do business with Japanese banks. You have to necessarily open an account with a local Japanese bank, as some companies make and accept payments through them only.

5. "Made in Japan" is the Best:

The Japanese clearly think they make the best products in the world. So, in general, their first preference is "Made in Japan" products. Only if there is no option of a Japanese brand would they opt for another make. So, selling your products to other Japanese companies is easy if you are a sales manager in a Japanese company in India. In the initial days, the Japanese company I worked for, its brand name in India, was not as famous as it is today. So, our first target to sell our products was other Japanese companies operating in India, and for a particular niche product, this approach helped us achieve initial success. Similarly, when we had to purchase cars for our company's use, our first choice was a Toyota, though Toyota was expensive and did not have a large footprint in India.

6. Japanese are the Best:

Japanese people generally feel that their fellow Japanese are the best. In fact, the notion of "Made in Japan" being the best stems from this belief. Though the Japanese come across as humble people who have a lot of respect for others, close and extended interactions with Japanese people will reveal that the Japanese have a sense of superiority about themselves. The notion of them being the best leads to patronising behaviour by the Japanese towards other nationalities.

7. Japanese are the most Trustworthy:

Alongside the belief that the Japanese are the best comes the idea that only the Japanese can be trusted. Japanese do not trust others so easily. Building trust with the Japanese is challenging and takes a lot of time. This is why Japanese companies do not opt for joint ventures with foreign companies unless there is no other option. For the same reason, you will find that Japanese companies would only have a Japanese national as the head of their subsidiaries outside Japan with the authority to sign cheques firmly with that person. Though this is now changing, you will still find most Japanese companies headed by Japanese people, even in India. Again, due to their belief that the Japanese are the best and most trustworthy, it is rare that you will find a non-Japanese heading a Japanese company globally. When the top Japanese automaker Nissan announced Carlos Ghosn, a Brazilian person of French/Lebanese origin, as the Chairman and CEO of Nissan in 2001, it raised the eyebrows of business analysts worldwide in general and Japanese in particular. Probably, the belief of the Japanese that others cannot be trusted stood vindicated when Ghosn was arrested for cases of impropriety as the head of Nissan.

Not trusting other nationals also comes in the way of the growth of Japanese companies, particularly in the context of crucial investment decisions. For instance, a Japanese company will seldom take a call to invest, say, in India, in setting up its subsidiary or a manufacturing facility unless the proposal is first made by a Japanese and then vetted by other Japanese. This also can happen only after they come to India, spend time in what they call a market survey and do the smell test by themselves. While they may go by published reports on India regarding how the economy is faring and so on, a final decision on investment will be taken only after it is recommended by the Japanese and approved by Japanese management.

The so-called market survey is most likely to include meetings with Japanese staff based in India in other Japanese companies (maybe even competitors) and, more importantly, with Japanese teams in the Japanese banks based in India to get first-hand feedback on the Indian experience, problems they encounter and so on. These meetings also help them understand the living conditions, like housing, schools, food, general living conditions, etc., for the Japanese in India and the precautions the Japanese staff needs to take to live in India. I know for a fact Japanese who are going to be based in India on a long-term basis go through a round of health check-ups and preventive vaccination doses for different diseases. (As an aside, Japanese staff posted in countries outside Japan are paid a "Hardship allowance," which depends on the country's nature and their salaries.)

The extent to which the Japanese prepare themselves to live in other countries reveals their risk-averse nature. I don't think nationals of different nations go to this extent to prepare themselves.

8. Lifelong Employment for Japanese:

Though this aspect has changed since the dawn of this millennium, most Japanese, even today, start work in one company and retire from it. While based on the competence of the individual, the pace of career growth varies, a Japanese employee rarely gets fired from a Japanese company. One may think this kind of job security may encourage employee complacency. Here's the paradox that I found very interesting. Even though they have high job security, the Japanese are stressed the most at work. They take their assigned jobs very seriously and get stressed too much regarding the position.

In Japan, about 53.3 percent of employees felt strongly troubled by their current working situation as of 2021, down from 54.2 percent in 2020, as per a report[4]. Within the last decade, figures for employees feeling severely insecure and stressed within their working environment peaked in 2012, reaching almost 61 percent. As a corollary, it is also common for Japanese employees to excessively smoke, drink, play *Pachinko* (Gambling machines), and visit *Karaoke* rooms and bars as a matter of relieving their work-related stress. In summary, the employer-employee equation in Japan is mutual. The employees stick to a company by and large for life, and employers do not sack or fire their staff, come what may. I must add that Japanese companies provide lifelong employment only for their Japanese team. In other countries, they do not have qualms about sacking people due to performance and in the same way the other nationals do not stay loyal to their companies so much.

9. Japanese are Generalists and Multi-functional:

One of the interesting aspects of the Japanese I noted was that they are generalists and multi-functional. This means that a typical Japanese person, regardless of educational or functional background, can easily pick up another function and perform satisfactorily. In Japanese companies, you will find that staff are rotated in diverse positions every three years, from sales to procurement, logistics to marketing, administration to production planning, and so on. Except for core and specialised functions like design, engineering, and finance, the Japanese believe in continuous job rotation for their staff. I think there are a few reasons why the Japanese can manage to do this successfully. First, Japan has the highest IQ level in the world[5], so they are sharp at picking up new things. Second, they are very logical in their thinking approach. This emerges from the Japanese *"Gembaism"*[6] system, combining intuitive, rational, and holistic thinking through experience. The belief is that if a person is trained naturally to think logically in any given situation, he can fit in any role, apply the thinking technique, and perform exceptionally well. I have seen this myself with many Japanese who keep shifting positions every three years and still perform well. Third, Japan follows a very homogeneous education system. In the words of one of my ex-Japanese colleagues, the education system in Japan is like inserting a round pipe into a chopping machine. It just ejects out multiple concentric rings of the same diameter and shape. What he meant was the output from a school or college was very homogenous. Because of this homogeneous system, Japanese are trained to be generalists and can quickly pick up on the job. In summary, because of their higher IQ levels, their logical thinking process, and the fact that they are generalists, it is possible for the Japanese to be multi-functional and successful.

Now, the above points can be turned on their heads and used to critique the Japanese education system. The homogeneous system also doesn't augur well for fostering diversity in thinking and creativity – one of the reasons why we don't find many success stories from Japan in the new technology internet space.

10. Commitment to the Consumer:

The one aspect of Japanese companies that has kept them in good stead is their unwavering commitment to the consumer. In decision making, the consumer's interest comes first and then the organisation's, even if it costs the organisation. I feel this is an aspect Indian companies could learn from the Japanese.

11. Decision making by Consensus:

In Japan, decisions are made by reaching a consensus among all people concerned. This is another reason for the slow decision making among the Japanese apart from their low-risk appetite. Every issue involves discussions involving stakeholders who go through the problem from their angle and come up with their observations. Much of the observations veer around risk mitigation, which, as mentioned before, is the cornerstone of decision making. This conventional decision-making style in the Japanese system, which is bottom-up and consensus-driven, is called the *Ringi*[7] system. *"Rin"* means submitting a proposal to one's superior and obtaining approval; *"gi"* means deliberations and decisions. This word, in a sense, conveys the essence of the Japanese decision-making style. When a consensus is reached, the issue is discussed threadbare, everyone is on board, and there is no looking back. For example, once Japanese companies want to invest in a particular market, they will take their time to analyse and decide, but once they have chosen, they will be in the market for the long term. While consensus in decision making exists, in my personal experience, I have noted that the team builds consensus around what the boss has in mind. In this sense, it is no different from an authoritative decision-making mode. So, yes, the Japanese decide by consensus, but after knowing what the boss has in mind!

While on this, an exciting anecdote comes to my mind. When you make a business proposal to the Japanese and if it is not acceptable, they seldom say "No" to your face. The most likely answer will be *We will consider,"* (pronounced as Konshider). So, one of my ex-Japanese bosses told me that when a Japanese says "Consider," it actually means "No!"

12. Ethics and Value Systems:

When you work in a Japanese company, you will get an idea of the importance the Japanese attach to ethics. Japanese companies are known to follow strong ethics and shun shortcuts to achieve growth. Apart from this, they also follow strong work ethics like being punctual, giving respect to customers, employees, and people in general, and paying salaries on time to employees come what may. Again, my Ex-boss, when I was the Country Manager for India, told me during induction that salaries to staff must be paid on the committed payday, come what may, and if required, supplier payments can be delayed but never the salaries. The punctuality of the Japanese is now part of folklore; hence, I have nothing much to add. Similarly, the obsession of the Japanese with cleanliness and, more importantly, being organised is also well-documented and known.

13. The Buck stops at the Top:

Another commendable aspect of Japanese management is how top management takes ownership of any mistake. It is not very uncommon to see the CEO or the Top Executive of a Japanese company coming to a press conference and bending their head to the front literally to apologise for the bad performance of their company in the previous year. I had witnessed this aspect of owning up by the boss in another situation in the company where I worked. Similarly, when we had to terminate a distributor, my Japanese MD, who is typically not involved in all customer meetings, volunteered to come for the meeting to break the news. In another instance, during the Global Financial Crisis, when we had to lay off a few people, the MD stood in front to break the news to each employee instead of leaving it to HR or the immediate functional superior.

14. Product Comes First and Marketing Later:

Being logical thinkers, the Japanese attach utmost importance to the product, its features, its benefits, how it can be better than the competition, its value proposition, and its price-performance positioning. They believe that for a company to be successful, its products and how customers receive them are at the core. Therefore, marketing is not a priority, unlike the Americans who attach much importance to marketing. Marketing has to do more with emotion rather than logic, so in terms of priority, it doesn't appear in the pecking order. The reason the Japanese are not market leaders in some categories despite having the best products may be this relatively lesser importance attached to marketing.

I understand that in the last twenty years or so, the Japanese attitude towards marketing has changed, and the Japanese are warming up to the importance of marketing. Yet, I feel that this is more a reaction out of compulsion and is not organic.

15. Strong Belief in "Seeing is Believing":

An aspect of the Japanese I found very interesting is their obsession with "sights" and "visuals." When the Japanese visit a country on a business trip, you will see them feverishly clicking pictures of anything and everything. Their business trip reports will have fewer words and more pictures – not just about the business aspect but also about other sights. For example, when they visit India, I have found them often taking pictures of cows in the street, which they find very strange, of Indians consummately eating with their hands, which they find odd, and of slums and high rises side by side, which they find it difficult to fathom. By giving a flavour of all this in these market visit reports, they believe it becomes easy for all concerned to understand the overall market situation.

I suppose this stress on visually presenting and understanding things comes again from their education system. In several meetings, I found the Japanese using the board to write and understand all the time. Electronic boards were omnipresent in Japanese companies even in the 90s. Similarly, almost all Japanese are well versed in drawing the map of Japan while explaining their country to others and they like it if we do the same when explaining Indian geography.

Talking of "Seeing is Believing," in the Japanese company I was working for, we were working on establishing a wholly-owned subsidiary in India. A Japanese team proposed the same along with us but went through rounds of discussion without the top management nodding. Finally, the group's Chairman visited India, and we took him on a flying visit to key cities like Mumbai, Bengaluru, and Delhi. During this visit, which was back in 2006, he could see for himself the rapid changes in the economic landscape in India. He was particularly impressed with what he saw inside the campuses of some IT majors like Infosys in Bengaluru, including the mini-golf course, which he was quite impressed with. Right on his return to Japan, he gave the green signal to set up the sales subsidiary in India and chided his team for delaying it for so long! Bosses are bosses, you see!

The key traits of the Japanese style of management that define their way of doing business can be summarised as follows:

1. Long-term oriented
2. Low-risk appetite and High regard for safety
3. Slow but structured decision making
4. Flexibility is a No-No
5. Live by "Continuous Improvement"
6. Logical thinking, keeping emotions aside
7. Belief in Japan, Japanese and "Made in Japan" to be the best
8. The buck stops at the top
9. Strong belief in ethics and value systems
10. Conservative in budgeting

If the above characteristics of the Japanese give a fair idea of the Japanese style of Management, on the other end of the spectrum is the American style, which we will go through in the next chapter.

Chapter 3

American Style of Management

I had the opportunity to work for over a decade with an American multinational company and also interact with and observe the functioning of many American companies. Globally, American businesses have been highly successful, and therefore, the American style has been one of the most sought after for a long while until the Japanese companies started making an impact in America. One cursory look at the American style would reveal an almost 180-degree variation from the Japanese. Except for some common aspects, which I will detail, the American style is precisely opposite to the Japanese style. The fact that both styles have been successful for a sustained period indicates that there could be good aspects in both that others can imbibe.

American corporations have been visible symbols of capitalism, and therefore, the American style of management, in a sense, follows quite a few capitalist principles. At the same time, I also feel that a few general myths associated with the American management style need to be busted. The main feature of capitalism is the motive to make a profit. As Adam Smith, the 18th-century philosopher and father of modern economics, said: *"It is not from the benevolence of the butcher, the brewer, or the baker that we expect our dinner, but from their regard to their own interest.*[8] Capitalism is often thought of as an economic system in which private actors own and control property by their interests, and demand and supply dictate prices in markets to serve society's best interests.

An IMF paper on capitalism authored by Sarwat Jahan and Ahmed Saber Mahmud outlines its founding pillars as private property, self-interest, competition, market mechanisms, and freedom.

When we look at the critical aspects of the American style of management, they all take their origins from the above founding pillars of capitalism. In my opinion, they are:

1. Profits Only Matter:

Companies exist for profits or versions of it like EBIDTA (Earnings before Interest, Depreciation, Taxes and Amortisation). Whatever other tall objectives they profess in public, the single most significant motive for companies is profit only. In pursuit of this objective, American companies pursue aggressive growth targets in a favourable market situation, cut costs drastically in an unfavourable market situation, or pursue moderate growth and operate at optimal costs in a mixed market situation. Even certain lofty ideals like Corporate Social Responsibility Goals or Green Goals, which American companies pursue in a way, will be linked to the ulterior profit motive. There is another important reason for this single-minded focus on profits by American companies, which is covered in detail later in this chapter.

2. Short-term or Medium-term Orientation:

If an English economist and thinker, Lord Maynard Keynes[9] said, *"In the long run, we are all dead,"* it is the Americans who believe in it thoroughly. In general, Americans do not believe in the long term. So, decision making is always with a short-term or medium-term perspective. This is increasingly becoming the norm, particularly with investment decisions. Companies are reluctant to invest money or resources where the gestation period is more than three years. This is also becoming a vital issue in "Make" or "buy" decisions, in the sense that instead of investing in engineering/research and development, which may yield results in the long term, companies prefer to buy out designs or products off the shelf or acquire other entities which have ready-made products.

Similarly, Americans would only prefer to invest in markets that can give results right from the word go (therefore, mature markets) rather than markets that need nurturing to get results. For a non-American working in an American company in an evolving market like India, understanding and internalising this point is very important so that there is no frustration when business cases don't get management approval because they are too long term.

Because of this short-term approach, even strategic decisions are sometimes taken with a myopic view. For example, when the results are not good in a year, an American company may decide to shut its factory or operations on a whim, ignoring the long-term potential of the market or the kind of sunk investments. Another season, another management, and you will find the same company doing a re-launch into the same market, claiming that this is where the future potential is. The irony is not lost on anyone when the company has to rebuild everything from scratch in a market where it had built a substantial presence not too long ago. Ford's decision to exit the Indian market after the Covid pandemic is an example. We should not be surprised if Ford re-enters the Indian market in a few years. Cutting losses as an approach comes easy for Americans.

3. High Appetite for Risks:

In general, American companies are known to take risks. That doesn't mean that they are prone to taking blind risks. Interestingly, OLBG[10] (Online Betting Guide) reveals that the USA, in comparison to twenty other countries, was shown to have the most risk-taking residents. In an article on the American risk-taker, Julie Scheidegger writes that the American risk-taker's legacy is born out of exploration, oppression, democracy, and the promise of the American Dream. This explains the risk-taking nature of Americans.

We have many examples where American companies took significant risks and succeeded. Microsoft comes to my mind first. After faltering with a slew of mistakes on the mobile phone, Microsoft bet big on its gaming console – Xbox back in 2001. Today, it's not just a leader in gaming but also a major player in video streaming. Another example is Google, which put its money into a video service like YouTube in 2006. The rest, as they say, is history. A more recent example is Microsoft's bet on OpenAI's ChatGPT. I must add that we are talking in general about the American style of management. The individual approaches of companies toward handling risks may differ; therefore, there could be examples of American companies that didn't take many risks and missed opportunities.

4. Hire-and-Fire and then Hire:

I reckon this aspect of the American management style is very popular and most talked about. American companies add human resources and retrench at the drop of a hat. When things go wrong in the business, layoffs are among the top three actions an American company would take. Therefore, employee loyalty in American companies is also at a very low level. As far as handling human resources is concerned, American companies are the most detached and unemotional.

At the beginning of 2023, we witnessed a slew of layoffs in many large American companies, particularly in the technology sector. These layoffs have been massive and necessitated by the business slowdown since the last quarter of 2022. The irony is that most of these companies had gone on a hiring spree to handle the upswing in demand thanks to the work-from-home phenomenon amid the

COVID-19 pandemic that rocked the world in March 2020. With most of the commerce and other activities moving online, the tech sector was on a considerable upswing even when conventional businesses had to take a beating due to disruption in supply and reduction in demand. So, American companies did not bat their eyelids for hiring a few quarters ago in plenty to cater to the market boom and quickly resorted to firing later due to sagging demand. And one shouldn't be surprised if the same companies again get into a hiring mode by the end of this year on the back of a resurgent demand. American companies do not mind re-hiring the same people they let go during a layoff routine!

5. Outsource and Outsource:

When there was a time when companies believed in doing it all by themselves due to IP (Intellectual Property) concerns, it was the American companies who started the trend of outsourcing. Outsourcing as an organised phenomenon began in the '70s and '80s when American companies started thinking that they should just focus on their core activities and strengths like design, technology, Marketing, and so on and outsource routine activities like administration and back-office functions and processes to stay agile and more importantly cut costs and improve profits. This again ties back to the principles of capitalism.

Over time, companies have constantly explored more and more areas to outsource, and outsourcing IT-enabled services has opened up a huge opportunity for a country like India. Today, American companies outsource accounting, HR/Payroll functions, Administration, Maintenance, IT, Call centres, Customer support, Warehousing, Logistics, Legal, etc.

When labour costs rose in America in the '90s, American companies started outsourcing production to other countries – mainly China. The word "Shanghaied" was born. In the first decade of this millennium, when American companies began outsourcing software development to companies in Bengaluru, the term "Bangalored" came into being.

I also find American firms to be the most open to engaging external consultants. Their openness to outsourcing is in sync with their risk-taking character and focus on profits.

6. Being Open, Flexible, and Quick to embrace anything new:

Being open to new ideas and initiatives is one extremely positive attribute among American managers. This aspect of American business has kept the country in good stead as a harbinger of hope to seekers of the American Dream. There are so many who got stifled in their own countries but could come up with new ideas in America and prosper.

The other welcome aspect of American companies is that they are flexible in their approach. They are not dogmatic in their thought processes, allowing them to follow a system that works best in a situation. For instance, when American companies operate in other countries, they are flexible to adapt to the local culture and fine tune their offerings instead of being rigid about their philosophy. Look at McDonald's strategy in India. McDonald's, whose claim to fame in America is its flagship product – the hamburger, does away with the same in its menu in recognition of the local cultural sensitivities. Similarly, in Ahmedabad, Gujarat, where people are predominantly vegetarian, there is a McDonald's outlet that serves only vegetarian fare.

American companies are also quick to embrace anything new. This comes from being open to new ideas and flexible to try new things.

7. Being at the Forefront of Innovation:

The reason behind America's consistent success over the years is its quest for innovation. If the Japanese have "Continuous

Improvement" in their core, the Americans have "Continuous Innovation" in theirs. In an article[11] written for usnews.com, Gary Shapiro attributes the following five central elements that set the US apart from the rest of the world as a beacon of innovation:

- The First Amendment of America's constitution that protects free speech.
- The culture of American exceptionalism that encourages risk-taking.
- America, being a nation of immigrants that welcomes and takes in people from around the globe.
- America's education system that values exploration and out-of-the-box thinking over rote learning.
- America's public policy framework which has traditionally favoured entrepreneurship, small businesses, and start-ups.

If you look around, particularly in the technology domain, American companies have been at the forefront of innovation and have created game-changing, disruptive products and solutions, whether it is a search engine like Google, an electric car like Tesla, or a taxi-hailing app like Uber.

However, America has lost its leadership position in innovation in the last few years to smaller countries like Israel that are feverishly catching up. However, it is still head and shoulders above many other developed countries.

8. Quick Decision making:

In the American management style, speed is of utmost importance. American companies are rapid in decision making. They believe in making decisions quickly rather than sitting on an issue. So, as far as I have seen, procrastination is not in the DNA of Americans. Instead, they would take a chance with a wrong decision rather than not decide at all. This is an aspect in which American companies tend to make tactical short-term decisions that may be detrimental to the business. Since the focus is on speed, the big picture is not often seen; long-term implications are not thought out, enough consultations do not happen among all stakeholders and decisions are taken on the whim. This holds even for critical issues like laying off people, thumbing down on investments, winding up businesses, shutting down product lines, etc.

An excellent example of this attribute of American companies is what happened with Sam Altman at Open AI. On 17 November 2023, Open AI fired its founder and CEO, Sam Altman. Can you imagine that by 20 November, the board reinstated him as CEO? In the interim, Altman also joined Microsoft.

9. It's All About Marketing, Baby:

For Americans, Marketing is among the key priorities in running a business. As a corollary, Americans are some of the best marketing and communication minds. There are examples galore of how so many American companies have been globally successful due to a strong marketing strategy. In aspects of marketing, Americans are the last to take any shortcuts. They understand the power of a brand very well and weave their marketing campaigns around building the consumer's emotional connection with the brand.

Americans have been pioneers in creative and imaginative marketing campaigns over the years. In this aspect, America leads, and the world follows. Unsurprisingly, some of the best All-Time marketing campaigns in history, like those of Nike (Just Do It), Apple (Get A Mac), and The Marlboro Man, are all of American origin.

You can see that Americans have extended the concept of marketing not just in product marketing but also on the political stage. In recent memory, the campaign by Barack Obama in 2007-08 for his presidential contest is seen as a trailblazer for political campaigns worldwide.

10. From One Quarter to Another:

Unlike the Japanese, we have already seen that Americans are very short-term oriented. It is so short term that companies decide everything on a quarter-to-quarter basis. Even a spectacular result in the previous quarter doesn't matter if the current quarter is not going well. American management leaders immediately get into course correction mode based on the results from the immediate past quarter. I believe this fixation with quarter performances is a bane for the American management style as it makes the entire organisation live by the quarter without any medium-term or long-term orientation.

In American companies, I have seen that when the results of the immediate past quarter are not good, the executive management is under tremendous pressure to announce some drastic corrective measures during the review meeting with the board. The management feels that they will have to demonstrate that they can make tough decisions when the going is not good, and retrenchment is the first manifestation of that.

Similarly, despite clearly laid out full-year marketing plans and spending plans, if the results in the previous quarter are not good, marketing spending for the subsequent quarters is reduced. To a large extent, this also works as a demotivating factor for the team, vendors, and, at times, customers when some planned customer-impacting initiatives are put on hold.

11. Personal Priorities over Company Priorities:

Due to the long history of capitalistic influence in American companies, there is a tendency for managers in American companies to put their personal interests before the organisation's. The pay structure in American companies is highly skewed towards individual performance bonuses, which makes employees go all out to achieve their individual goals and maximise their bonuses.

In the bargain, this also leads to unscrupulous and unethical activities by employees, which can hamper the business in the long run. More often than not, I have noticed that employees are happy to achieve their goals while not being concerned about the company's goals. This philosophy permeates many American companies' hierarchy from the bottom to the top.

Some of the mega scandals in the world in recent memory, like Enron, Theranos, and, more recently, FTX, all involve American companies. In this context, who can forget this immortal quote by Jacob Frenkel, Vice Chairman of AIG, in 2008? *The left side of the balance sheet (Assets) has nothing right, and the right side of the balance sheet (liabilities) has nothing left. But they are equal to each other. So, accounting-wise, we are fine!"*

12. Open and Fair Work Culture:

American society is most open, and so are American companies. Again, driven by capitalistic principles, American companies attach much importance to meritocracy. Therefore, unlike Japanese or Korean companies, you will see many American corporations being headed by non-Americans as well, which is seen as no big deal at all. A Sundar Pichai heading Google or a Satya Nadella heading Microsoft is neither by luck nor by chance. The advocacy of diversity and being open to talent from anywhere are the main reasons for the success of American companies. So, if you are capable and in the right place at the right time, you can become the CEO of an American corporation, notwithstanding your origins.

American companies are open, which is why you will find a less formal work culture in them than in others. The dress culture is semi-formal or casual, depending on the industry, and there is an all-prevailing first-name culture across the organisation. Business meetings in America are formal and to the point. There is no general beating around the bush. Meetings start on time, but the ending depends on whether the objective has been achieved.

There is a general myth that American companies are unfair to their employees. This notion probably has to do with the way American companies hire and fire people. But in my experience, I have found American companies to be extremely fair in sticking to agreements and contracts. They may not be seen to be overly empathetic to customers, vendors, and employees and are likely to be seen as ruthless and looking after their own interests. This is, to some extent, true, though American companies tend to go by the written word entirely without dilly-dallying on the same unless more significant issues are at play. For employees, the hire-and-fire approach is a huge dampener, but American companies do abide by the severance rules of the country.

I also noticed that many of the HR policies in American companies are highly progressive compared to other countries. In America, the current trend is not to ask the candidate about their last drawn salary while hiring - a practice that is so common in India. A company has to make an offer based on its budget or what it feels is the market rate for the role. Similarly, American companies do not delve too much into the candidate's family background and stick to professional background checks while hiring.

13. Aggressive in Approach and Outlook:

If the Japanese are conservative in their outlook, the Americans are the opposite. In general, American companies want to achieve more and more in less and less time. So, in a planning exercise, American companies tend to be over-optimistic. The headwinds are considered but are augmented with a set of mitigation plans that are sometimes impractical. In the same measure, American companies do not wait eternally for all the elements in the external business environment to be conducive to starting their business. Even if seven out of ten issues are clear, they would like to jump in and work towards sorting out the balance of three issues later. Understanding this approach becomes important for non-Americans who want to work in American companies as this would help them to be in sync with the management approach during budgeting and planning.

14. Americans are Domain Specialists:

Americans tend to be specialists in their domains and dig deep over time. So, they avoid spreading themselves thin across unrelated or even related domains and are unapologetic about it. This goes against the Japanese way, where they are seen as generalists. By the same token, Americans would like to deal with things that are uncluttered rather than jumping into something that is, at the outset, complicated.

15. Individualistic in Decision Making:

In American companies, the decision-making style is more individualistic. Managers tend to discuss with their subordinates and obtain consensus, which is not binding on the final decision. They tend to go by their thinking and take accountability for the decisions taken in their sphere of control. If the decision flops, the managers are made to pay the price, and at the same time, when it works, they are handsomely rewarded as well. It is also said that American managers tend to ignore or disregard the opinions of their team members and stick to their own decisions. This, of course, spoils the spirit of working together as a team, but that's how it is.

In summary, the following ten traits summarise the American style of management:

1. Highly driven by capitalistic principles
2. Individualistic
3. Aggressive in approach and outlook
4. High-Risk appetite
5. Short-term to Medium-term thinking
6. Innovation-driven
7. Marketing and Branding focus

8. Open and Fair
9. Quick decision making
10. Flexible to the core

An internal guiding principle statement of Nike, the American footwear company, sums up the American way of management or doing business in general. And here it goes:

1. *"Our business is Change.*
2. *We're on offence. All the time.*
3. *Perfect results count – Not a perfect process. Break the rules: Fight the law.*
4. *This is as much about battle as about business.*
5. *Assume nothing. Make sure people keep their promises. Push yourselves to push others. Stretch the possible.*
6. *Live off the land.*
7. *Your job isn't done until the job is done.*
8. *Dangers: Bureaucracy, Personal ambition, Energy takers Vs Energy givers, Knowing your weakness, Don't get too many things on the platter."*

Chapter 4

Indian Style of Management

"Indians run businesses like families and families like businesses!"

– Narayana Murthy, Founder and Ex-Chairman, Infosys

Has the Indian style of management evolved, or is it still a work in progress?

Is the Indian management style inspired by the scriptures like it is believed to be?

Is the Indian style of management indigenous, or is it imbibed from other styles?

India is a diverse country where the language, dialect, food habits, dressing style, beliefs, and culture change every few hundred kilometres. In such a heterogeneous environment, is there scope for defining one single management style?

In the coming sub-chapters, as we discuss various aspects of the Indian management style, we will attempt to answer these questions. But before that, let us first briefly look at the history of management in India and the popular styles within India based on different communities and regions that provide context to the larger Indian style of management.

Chapter 4A

History of Management in India

India, a country with an ancient civilisation and history, possesses rich sources of material from which we can gain knowledge on multiple subjects, including management. This includes:

Chanakya's *Arthashastra*[12]:

Some early references to management in the history of India can be found in *Arthashastra*, written by Kautilya, also known as Chanakya or Vishnu Gupta. Written in 323 BC, *Arthashastra* is a discourse on governance and administration given to the then Maurya King Chandragupta. However, the scope and pertinence of the ideas are such that they have invariably found their way into management as well. This should be considered the first documented treatise on management practices written in an instructional format for the King.

In this work, Chanakya outlines the need to govern through *Prabhu Shakti* (Vision), *Mantra Shakti* (Mission), and *Utsah Shakti* (Motivation). Another important issue he stresses in detail is the need for a well-defined organisation in the kingdom where roles and responsibilities are clearly defined. Chanakya then goes on to define a set of processes for each governance function. There are other essential suggestions that Chanakya provides as part of this manual for governance to the King. Today, Chanakya is celebrated as a man of solid wisdom who could think ahead of his time. Many books and materials that also revere the contents of *Arthashastra* and claim to be, in a way inspired by the thinking of modern-day management gurus like Peter Drucker, are available. The moot question is whether the day-to-day functioning of Indian businesses in any way is inspired by the teachings of Chanakya. In my opinion, while, as Indians, we would like to celebrate and take pride in Chanakya and his treatise, the jury is still out on whether we took any lessons from his work to our businesses and management styles on a day-to-day basis.

Vedas:

The *Vedas* are a set of very ancient scripts in Sanskrit from 1500 BC to 900 BC, with their origins in India. The *Vedas*, which means knowledge, have one part called the *Upanishads* that discuss aspects related to spiritual knowledge. Therefore, there is a possibility that some wisdom associated with managing affairs is imparted in these texts, though there are no direct references. In his book *Arthashastra*, Chanakya talks about six lessons from the *Vedas*[13] for governance. These are *Vasudeva Kutumbakam* (World is a family), *Samarpan Bhav* (Dedication), *Lokasangraha* (Welfare of all beings), *Shubh Labh* (Ethical Profits), *Nishkama Karma* (Deeds without greed), and *Ati Hayastha Varjayet* (Shunning Extremes). Among these principles, I can see that Indian businesses traditionally practice two or three of them. These are *Lokasangraha* (Welfare of all beings and, in the context of business, the welfare of the staff), *Shubh Labh* (Ethical Profits), and *Ati Hayastha Varjayet* (Shunning Extremes). We will delve into more details of these when we discuss some key traits of the Indian management style in the coming chapters.

Epics – Ramayana and Mahabharata

A cursory search on the internet for management lessons from Indian mythological epics like *Ramayana* and *Mahabharata* and Hindu texts like *Bhagavad Gita* yields a lot of interesting perspectives. Though the original material may not directly refer to running a company or a business, there have been derivations and interpretations to arrive at conclusions. For instance, in *Mahabharata*, the way Arjuna takes Krishna as his mentor, despite himself being a capable warrior, serves as a lesson in management on tapping the right people as mentors to help run a business or industry. Similarly, in *Ramayana*, Ram utilises the services of Vibhishan, the brother of his adversary Raavan, to understand his opponent's strengths and weaknesses on the battlefield. This is a lesson on how to tap into the resources of your competitors while facing them in the marketplace. Having said that, I wouldn't say that on a day-to-day basis, Indian managers refer to these ancient texts for answers while facing business situations.

With this in perspective, let us look at the recent evolution of Indian management in business.

Evolution of Indian Management:

My submission is that the history of Indian management as we practice today, doesn't extend far into the past. As Dr Subhash Sharma, professor at the Indus Business Academy, postulates in his paper titled "Evolution of Indian Management – Towards a new paradigm of knowledge creation in Management and Leadership,[14]" the evolution of the Indian style of management can be grouped into six phases and I quote:

"Phase 1 started in the 1960s and 70s by replicating Western Management models and ideas. This phase was referred to as 'Management in India' and dealt with how effectively Western Models were implemented in the Indian context.

Phase 2 occurred when some scholars and researchers from IIMs and outside started exploring Indian concepts in management. This marked the beginning of the introduction of Indian concepts in management, which can be termed integrative indigenisation.

In Phase 3 in the 1990s, an attempt was made to connect management and culture, partly inspired by Japanese management. This was followed by linking management with human values and Indian scriptures.

In Phase 4, between the 1990s and 2000, Indian ideas in management spread. The concept of management was changed and expanded to link it with the idea of development.

In Phase 5, research in Indian management gained momentum. Globalising Bharatiya Management/Indian Management is central to this idea.

Phase 6, which is the present, looks towards the future when Indian Management ideas will spread globally."

As appealing as these phases of management and the evolving picture appear, the study is more from an academic perspective as to how academicians have explored the evolution of Indian management. In my opinion, the evolution of management can be grouped into the following phases:

Phase 1 (Up to the 1960s and 1970s): A combination of adopting British processes, American style in bits and pieces, and undocumented traditional Indian styles. Thanks to the long British rule in India, many British companies operated in the country, and by default, they followed British processes. A few American companies established businesses in India, either on their own or as joint ventures with Indian companies, thereby automatically imparting their management techniques to local companies. Examples include American companies like IBM and Coca-Cola, which entered India early. However, they had to exit in the 1970s due to government policies and re-entered after the 1990s.

Phase 2 (1980s and 1990s): Pre-liberalisation and post-liberalisation period when Indian companies were keen to improve their management practices by learning from the Japanese and Americans. During this period, once the Indian economy was opened up to foreign competition, many Indian groups quickly collaborated with foreign companies to introduce their products into India. This was when awareness of Quality management theories in production like TQM (Total Quality Management) and ISO certification was high among Indian companies. This naturally led to the internalisation of global management techniques not just in manufacturing but in overall management as well. An excellent example is Rank Xerox, which tied up with the BK Modi group and launched photocopiers under the aegis of Modi Xerox Ltd. Modi Xerox could access the legendary direct-selling model of Rank Xerox worldwide. This, in turn, helped spread the same techniques and tools to other direct-selling companies too.

Phase 3 (2000 to 2020): Emergence of *desi* management techniques and a strong confluence of other management styles. During this period, as the Indian economy became part of the emerging global economies, a few native management concepts gained fame and received international attention. I would like to talk about a few of these indigenous ideas.

1. Entry of *Jugaad* into the global management lexicon:

    It is in this period that *Jugaad,* which is a Hindi term for a quick-fix low-cost solution, became branded as "The Great Indian *Jugaad,*" signifying a frugal and flexible way to innovation by authors Jaideep Prabhu and Navi Radjou in their book. We will look at this aspect in more detail in a separate chapter.

2. Mumbai *Dabbawallas* Become Harvard Case Study Material[15]:

    Mumbai *Dabbawallas* are an army of over 5000 men dressed in traditional white outfits with Gandhi caps who deliver home-cooked food to an estimated 200,000 office-goers from home to office daily on time at their offices in the commercial capital city of Mumbai in India. In 2010, Stefan Thomke published a case study co-authored with Mona Sinha for the Harvard Business School on Mumbai *Dabbawallas* titled "The *Dabbawalla* System: On-time Delivery, Every Time". In that case study, the authors say that the *Dabbawalla* system achieves a very high service performance (Six Sigma equivalent or better) with a meagre cost and a straightforward operating system. The *Dabbawallas* and their unique model became so talked about that the British Royals invited them to visit the United Kingdom.

3. The Fortune at the Bottom of the Pyramid[16]:

    Originally published as a paper by Management Guru C.K. Prahalad and Stuart Hart in the business journal Strategy+Business, the concept was developed into a book with the same title. The book is a compilation of case studies of businesses that have succeeded by providing goods and services to the bottom of the economic pyramid. The concept caught attention because it went against the conventional thought of focusing on the top of the economic pyramid to maximise profits. Most of the case studies showcased Indian examples like Dabur, Cavincare, Hindustan Unilever, etc., where these companies innovated by launching SKUs (Stock Keeping Units) specifically targeted towards the poor yet, selling huge volumes and, in the bargain, meeting twin objectives of achieving profits and bringing in social equality. This is a native Indian concept that is now being taken to other economies with per capita incomes similar to India's.

4. The One Lac Rupee Nano Car:

When Ratan Tata, the then Chairman of the Tata Group, made it public in 2003 that his company was working on a Rs 1 lac (US$1250) car, everyone thought it was a fanciful idea that was not practical. The price of the lowest-priced car, the Maruti Alto, was 2.5 times more than this. Even a bike was priced close to Rs lac. The idea behind the pricing was to target an entirely new segment: the lower middle-class population in India commuting on a two-wheeler. Looking at the vast gap between the price of this proposed new car and the existing cheapest car in the market, the reaction was that of scepticism. When Tata actually displayed a functional Rs 1 lac priced car called the Tata Nano at the Auto Expo in Delhi in January 2008, the world was stunned and took serious notice of it. By July 2009, when the first deliveries of Nano happened, from initial disdain to later doubt to disbelief, the Nano project became a matter of national pride and international attention. Nano became a symbol of Indian capability – of being able to conceive, design, produce, market, and sell an innovative product at one-third the price by cutting the frills and maintaining efficiency through the supply chain. Nano, in short, demonstrated how the native frugal nature of Indians can be imbued into a commercial product.

Even outside the automotive industry, companies worldwide started thinking of a "Nano" model for their product categories to see if that could be accomplished, and the market expanded beyond the existing price-performance equations. Unfortunately, Nano failed to take off in the market after the initial flutter. The teething problems took a permanent toll on the safety and reliability image of the product. More than that, the initial positioning of the product based on price turned out to be a major folly. After the starting woes concerning product performance and marketing, Nano could not get the needed traction and had to be withdrawn from the market in 2018. Notwithstanding this failure, the launch of Tata Nano was a moment of glory, though short-lived for Indian management.

5. Amul – The Taste of India:

Before Nano, if one brand from India captured the world's imagination, it was Amul. Amul is a by-product of the White Revolution or the Milk Revolution that India undertook in the 1950s and 1960s, thanks to the cooperative movement in Gujarat. What started as a humble project to unite small dairy farmers is today a multi-billion-dollar industry involving over 3.5 million milk producers, making India the world's largest milk-producing country. Amul's story is about bringing together disparate farmers under a cooperative umbrella towards a common cause, scaling up quickly, managing complex operations efficiently, adopting some native marketing techniques, and finally, deftly marrying social and business objectives. Some of these aspects would become a mainstay of the Indian management style, which we will explore in the coming chapters. Today, Amul is not just the "Taste of India" but also the "Toast of India!"

Phase 4 (Current phase): Emergence of a Truly Indian Management Style:

In the period after 2020, which can be referred to as the current phase, we are witnessing the culmination of the evolution of the

Indian management style, whereby we are clearly able to define a set of distinct, identifiable characteristics. What are those traits, and what examples do we have to substantiate the presence of these traits? We will explore these in the upcoming chapters.

Chapter 4B

Diversity of Management Styles in India

"Whatever you can rightly say about India, the opposite is equally true."

– British Economist Joan Robinson

For namesake, India is one country. However, except for cricket, there is hardly anything that can commonly bind the entire country. It is like a union of many small countries (small in area but not necessarily in population), each defined by its own identity regarding culture, language, food, ethnicity, etc. After India gained Independence, the government divided the country into many states on a linguistic basis. Though not a fool proof method, it was, by and large, the most acceptable way of delineating the borders for different states within India. Therefore, the region containing people speaking the Tamil language became Tamil Nadu, the Marathi language became Maharashtra, and so on. In reality, is it so clearly demarcated just based on language? Not necessarily. This is just an example of how one cannot explain a phenomenon in India with a one-dimensional view. Conditions apply, and exceptions come into play.

Based on where people come from, an essential part of one's identity in India, they are grouped into specific communities. For example, people hailing from Gujarat belong to the Gujarati community, those from Punjab are Punjabis, those from Bengal are Bengalis, and so on. Among the various communities in India,

Gujaratis, Marwaris, Parsis, Sindhis, Jains, Punjabis, and Chettiars are known for their entrepreneurial spirit and business acumen. These communities have specific, unique characteristics that make them successful in business. Therefore, before defining the common management style of Indians, it will be interesting to see some of the traits of Gujaratis, Marwaris, Chettiars, and others concerning their way of doing business. Since richly documented material is available on these, we will not delve into detail but look at the salient features that will later be relevant when we draw the picture for the Indian management style.

The Gujarati Style of Doing Business:

The state of Gujarat is located along the Western coast of India, and the people who hail from this state are called Gujaratis or Gujjus in short. They speak the Gujarati language and its variants. In Gujarat, it is common for youngsters to start their own businesses instead of taking up employment. Unlike other states of India, this entrepreneurial streak also extends to women. One of the reasons for the success of the "White Revolution," or the cooperative movement spearheaded by Amul in the dairy industry in Gujarat, which we saw in the previous chapter, is that it also involved women in a big way.

During British rule, the East India Company used India as a sourcing hub for textiles, spices, tea, rubber, jute, etc., of which Gujarat supplied cotton goods, silk, and indigo. In fact, the British landed on the subcontinent through the port of Surat on August 24, 1604 AD, for trade. It is said that when the British colonists wanted to exit India, they sold their mills and businesses to local Gujarati traders. For example, the British sold the cloth mills to the "Mafatlals" of the Kheda District in Gujarat.

Gujaratis are, by nature, happy-go-lucky people who are fun-loving and like to live their lives king-size. They enjoy travelling and make up for a big chunk of tourists within India and abroad. Over 60%[17] of the population in Gujarat are vegetarians who abstain from all types of meat. Gujaratis are inherently risk-loving; therefore, you will find them actively engaging in speculative activities like trading in the stock market, forex trading, commodities trading, and even betting. Traditionally, Gujaratis don't believe in formal education as a means for advancement in life. Most Gujaratis do not pursue higher education and instead enter the family business as early as possible, which is one reason why you may find Gujaratis not so highly skilled in English communication. However, this has not stopped them from being successful in business as they possess an astute business sense as a community. Entrepreneurship is virtually a cultural obligation for Gujaratis and has consistently earned them the utmost respect. Starting a corner shop or a small business is seen as more important than holding a mid-level management job in someone else's company. Another well-known aspect of Gujaratis is that they are incredibly positive people who believe that the glass is always full.

Dhandha, or "business" in Hindi, is central to an average Gujarati's existence. They detest salaried, controlled 9-5 jobs but relish 9 – 9 *dhandha*. Gujaratis don't care much about work-life balance; for them, balancing the needs of *dhandha* with their domestic needs is more critical. No business is considered too small for them; every *dhandha* is good as long as there is profit in it. Doing business is ingrained in their DNA. In general, Gujarati believe in simple living and high thinking, which is why they typically lead a modest lifestyle and reinvest most of their earnings back into the business. While these stereotypes may no longer hold true for the coming generations, this attitude of dedicating oneself to *dhandha* defines a typical Gujarati.

There is an interesting trivia here. Business is so ingrained in the Gujarati community that some of the surnames of communities follow the business they do. Gold (*Zaver* in Hindi) merchants are *Zaveris/Jhaveris*, those who are brokers are *Dalals*, those in the cloth (*Kapda* in Hindi) business are *Kapadias*, those who keep accounts of money are *Nanavatis*, and so on. As an aside, when Putlibai, head of a Kapole business family, lent Rs 9,00,000 Lac (Nav Lakh) to the East India Company, their descendants were called *Navlakhis*.

"If you don't build your dream, someone else will hire you to help them build theirs." This quote, reportedly from Dhirubhai Ambani, the founder of the Reliance group, embodies the Gujaratis' business philosophy.

The common traits outlined above reflect how Gujaratis conduct their business. Some of the critical characteristics of the Gujarati way of doing business are as follows:

1. Fast Decision making:

    The Gujaratis are swift in decision making, which stems from being high-risk takers and relying on their instincts to make decisions. They are not the ones to keep thinking too deeply about a business proposal. Consequently, they also expect their business counterparts to be as quick in decision making. This creates, at times, frustration and misunderstanding when they deal with other cultures where decision making is not as quick.

2. Low-Cost Structure:

    The mantra of "Simple living" embodied in the Gujarati psyche is also extended to business. Gujarati promoters like to be seen as less flashy and maintain a low-cost structure that permits them to be agile and aggressively competitive.

3. Cost absorption Mantra:

    This is one thing I heard from a Gujarati businessman known to me. The gentleman said that when he was about to start his own business as a young boy in his early 20s, his father, on the very first day, outlined what should be his business philosophy in the trading business. In a month and every month, the first priority is to earn margins to cover interest first and then fixed cost. Once that is done, since everything else is clean profit, just focus on stock rotation. I could then understand how Gujarati traders could operate at very low margins at times when I understood this philosophy. By this philosophy, it is clear that in trading, stock rotation and cash flow take precedence over profits once costs are absorbed.

4. Quick and Prompt Payment Policy:

I have noticed that traditional Gujarati businessmen prioritise maintaining a clean track record when making payments. This might have changed with the current generation, but in general, Gujarati traders are particular in clearing their payments to their vendors and collecting payments from their customers, even if this means availing extra cash discounts for making early payments to vendors or extending cash discounts for collecting payments from customers.

5. Community Comes First:

The Gujarati community is a close-knit community in India, and no other group has such a strong sense of community as I have seen. In times of good and bad, the community comes together. I saw this when a devastating earthquake struck Kutch, Gujarat, in 2001. The entire Gujarati community rose to the occasion, wherever they were in the world, to support the rehabilitation efforts. In Gujarati businesses, the business is run like a closely held family, with the staff almost being treated like part of a large family. Traditionally, most of the finance to start a business comes from within the family or at least the community.

6. **In Gujaratis They Trust:**

Gujarati businessmen trust their fellow Gujaratis more and want to have them around in their businesses. Though this applies to all businesses, one example to drive home this point is the diamond polishing industry. Even today, in Surat, the global capital for diamond polishing, the promoters prefer to employ fellow Gujaratis from Palanpur whom they trust for carrying goods back and forth.

7. **Fearful and Greedy:**

The famous Warren Buffet's quote - *"Be fearful when others are greedy and be greedy when others are fearful"* - applies to the attitude of Gujaratis very well. This also explains the Gujaratis' liking for speculative trades like the stock market. It is said that one in every four Gujaratis invests in equity stocks.

8. **Networking to Grow the Biz:**

Gujaratis are adept at networking within the community to further their business interests. This networking also uses marriages to unite two families and expand the business empire.

9. **Long-term View of Business:**

Gujaratis generally have a long-term view of business and are not only in business for short-term profits. They believe in long-term wealth creation that extends across generations. You will find that most of the Gujaratis have been pursuing their family businesses for more than two or three generations while continuing to expand to newer horizons.

10. **Quick to Adapt to New Technologies:**

Though Gujaratis might not be ahead in formal education, they are incredibly sharp enough to understand and absorb new technologies. It is said that they may not be good at writing codes like the South Indians but are undoubtedly good at running companies that write codes.

These traits of Gujaratis have ensured that they are successful not just in India but in different parts of the world. The Gujarati community is among the first in India to leave the shores to pursue business in East Africa, the USA, Canada, and so on. In a piece[18] written by Neeraj Mahajan for the site – Taazakhabarnews, he mentions that Gujaratis, like the Jews, Chinese, English, Scots, and Lebanese, are among the most successful people in business, trade, or commerce in different parts of the world. They own more than one-third of hotels and motels in the United States. They own almost half of America's 12,000 independent pharmacies. 25% of the start-ups in Silicon Valley are founded by Gujaratis by birth and American citizens by marriage.

The Magic of Marwaris:

"Jahan Naa Pahunche Rail Gadi, Wahan Pahunche Bail Gadi, Aur Jahan Naa Pahunche Bail Gadi, Wahan Pahunche Marwari!" This famous saying which actually means that where the civilisation has just begun, a Marwari will start his business there, in a way embodies the spirit of Marwaris (Also called Marwadis colloquially). Though Marwaris represent an ethnic community from the Marwar region of Rajasthan, they are now present in almost all parts of India and, in a way, dominating certain lines of business. I am yet to come across another community that picks up local languages as quickly as the Marwaris. Similarly, they have the ability to blend in with the local culture without posing any threat to the locals. This crucial aspect has made the Marwari community warmly acceptable to the local community without conflicts wherever they go. These traits have made them an incredibly thriving business community known originally for their trading acumen and later manufacturing. Now, almost all spheres

of business, including E-commerce and Technology have a strong Marwari presence.

Like the Gujaratis, the Marwaris are also a close-knit community and follow a particular method of doing business, which can be outlined as follows:

1. Business runs in the Family, and Family runs in the Business:

    Most Marwari businesses are family-owned businesses where the family is the pillar of strength. In such a family structure, strict hierarchies are maintained according to age. The younger one doesn't question the elder one's wisdom in decision making concerning the business. The close tie within the family allows for empowerment, risk taking, and delegation. When I talk to my Marwari friends, many allude to the joint family system for their community's success in business.

    In his book, *"The Z-Factor: My Journey as the Wrong Man at the Right Time,"* well-known entrepreneur and industrialist Subhash Chandra of Zee group fame, who is a Marwari, talks about a ritual called *"Paani mein namak daalna."* This is a sacred vow taken within the Marwari trading communities, by which once you agree to do something during this ritual, you cannot back out.

2. Money Matters:

    One of the critical aspects of the Marwari business style is having absolute control over money matters. Wake up a Marwari businessman or, for that matter, a Marwari professional CEO from sleep and ask him about finances; he can reel off his assets, liabilities, and cash flow. In fact, most of the traditional Marwari companies, even today, follow the *"Parta"* accounting system by creating a daily

Profit and Loss (P&L) statement at the end of the day. It is like a daily health check for the business.

Marwaris are adept at strategic management of funds and investments. They are generally proactive in shifting investments to avenues that yield more productive returns while maintaining a very healthy short-term cash flow. One after effect of this trait is that in Marwari companies or businesses, you will mostly find a Marwari family man as the head of finance, ensuring highly controlled and centralised finance management.

3. The "KanJews" Marwari:

In India, it is very common to address someone who is very tight with his purse as a *"Kanjoos Marwari."* Marwaris are known to be highly conservative about their spending and wear this trait as a badge of honour. It is not in their genes to spend money on fads and flashiness. For a Marwari, every expense is treated as an investment, which means it has to give a return. This nature of controlling expenses tightly helps them to tide over any tough business cycle. A Marwari friend who is in the US told me that he calls himself "KanJews Marwari" in jest alluding to Jews, which is another community that knows their businesses and money. Here, I must add that there are three occasions for which Marwaris spend lavishly – Births, Marriages and Deaths. This is a paradox for the otherwise spendthrift Marwaris. This is because these occasions, especially marriages, are seen as opportunities to build social ties and display creditworthiness to the business community at large. This is their way of building social capital.

4. Wealth Creation by Business Expansion:

The basic philosophy that embodies a Marwari business is wealth creation that too, long term. Therefore, spotting opportunities even when they are not obvious and investing in them comes to them naturally. This, combined with their nature of taking risks regarding investments, is a proposition that is not easy to match. The motive of long-term wealth creation by jumping into the right opportunities and taking risks has made many Marwari companies diversify into unrelated businesses and succeed. In India, you have examples of many Marwari business houses that have diversified entirely from one end to another, like the Birlas, the Goenkas, The Agarwals, and so on. Though traditionally, Marwaris were known for the pawnbroking and jewellery business, today, you will find them running diverse businesses with aplomb. In fact, in the IT Hardware business, which I was personally associated with, I was surprised to see the Marwari community dominating it in almost every city in India. Though many of the businessmen didn't come into the business with very high formal education, the Marwari business people showed tremendous acumen in picking up the nuances of technology and the quick changes better than even technically qualified people.

5. The Marwari game of High Volume, Low Margin:

The underpinning philosophy of the Marwari business is to go after high volumes even at low margins. Because of their penchant for keeping costs low, they could afford to be extremely aggressive on pricing when it comes to trading. They focus on volumes, increasing revenue, keeping inventory to the minimum, and having a smooth cash rotation system. Beyond the breakeven levels, which are low due to the lower cost structure, their objective is to increase profits rather than be unduly anxious about the profit ratio.

6. **Unreasonable Negotiation in the Business as a Birth Right:**

    In my experience, I found Marwari businessmen to be the toughest when it comes to negotiations. In my conversations, they openly admitted that they consider being unreasonable in a business negotiation to be their birthright. It is a trait that has been imbibed into them from childhood. This is an interesting quote made to me by a Marwari business friend which sums up this aspect: *"Every day when I get up in the morning, I pray to God to make my day the best by getting the highest prices from my customers and the lowest costs from my suppliers!"*

7. **Treasuring Age and Experience:**

    Persisting with old and experienced people is a Marwari trait. Others may see this as a disadvantage because it comes at the expense of youth and fresh blood. However, over some time, it has served the Marwaris well. In Marwari companies, people in critical positions continue forever till they pass away or, for health reasons, cannot continue. Because of this famous tradition of respecting elders among Marwaris, experienced people are not asked to retire or leave. This is a trend changing for sure of late. In fact, Kumar Mangalam Birla, the Chairman of the Birla group, said that one of the early reforms he undertook in his group after he took over the reins was to put an end to what he called the "Womb-to-Tomb" policy and the unwritten rule that children of employees will automatically get jobs in the Birla group.

8. **Money Management as the only Core Competence:**

    Looking at the landscape of successful Marwari businesses in the country, like the Birlas, Khaitans, Goenkas, Dalmias, Jindals, and so on, it is often said that Marwaris don't believe in the concept of "Core Competence". Most of the above-said business groups are highly diversified and not necessarily in related businesses. It is possible that most of the Marwari Businesses started with commodity trading, which they feel is their core strength. Still, over some time, they have gotten into any business in which they see future wealth and value. But I would argue that there is one Core Competence that the Marwaris believe in and own, which is "Money Management."

Not surprisingly, many Chartered Accountants and MBA (finance) graduates are in the Marwari ranks today in many corporations. With their instinctive and inherent skill of managing finances skilfully, Marwaris believe that they can get into any business and still run it successfully by building the right team and artful delegation.

9. De-risking the business with Real estate investments:

In India, you will commonly find Marwaris investing their surpluses from business in real estate whenever they spot land availability at low prices. As real estate prices in India tend to only appreciate, and that too sharply depending on location and business cycles, Marwari businessmen use these investments to shore up their balance sheets. The strength of real estate assets in the balance sheet gives a sense of solidity to their companies' finances, which they leverage to get extended credit lines.

10. Philanthropy at the Heart of the Business:

While the aspect of Marwaris being tight with money is much talked about, what is not discussed much is their philanthropic activities. Most of the Marwari business groups allocate a portion of their wealth to social causes, mostly connected with their community through schools, colleges, hospitals, hostels, and temples.

I saw this interesting expansion of the term Marwari from the Twitter handle @nkmgmt that in a way, epitomises the Marwari business style.

M – Money, A - Accounting, R – Rigour, W- Wealth, A - Adjust, R – Risk Taking, I – Innovate

The Chettiars of the South:

The Chettiars[19] are a popular community that originated from Chettinad in Tamil Nadu. They were initially involved in trading precious stones but later became private money lenders and bankers. Like their counterparts in the North of Vindhyas, namely the Gujaratis and Marwaris, Chettiars also have a penchant for doing business and succeeding. They have an entrepreneurial mindset and are community-oriented, like the Gujaratis and Marwaris.

There are subgroups under Chettiars, namely Nagarathars, Naatukottai Chettiars, Devanga Chettiars, Telugu Chettiars, etc. Every community has unique characteristics that make them different yet successful. For example, the Nagarathars are considered pioneers of modern banking, and they introduced concepts like profit, loss, debit, credit, expenses and trial balance. They introduced the double-entry bookkeeping system and followed the 'Agency System.' Nattukottai Chettiars are traditional bankers and dominate foreign trade in Southeast Asian countries. However, the governmental restrictions on doing business in countries like Burma and Vietnam forced them to return to India, surrendering their assets.

Traditionally, Nagarathars believed in on-the-job training rather than formal education, and the sons will be trained in the firms of others before coming into their own family business. The practice of providing shares in business happens much later. Nagarathars' native instincts are to venture out and take risks, though the proportion of the community entering the business is reducing now. Regarding intrinsic competencies, Nagarathars are known for accounting practices, calculated risk-taking, trading and venturing into new markets, balancing business and philanthropy, integrity and self-reliance. Religious charity is an inborn characteristic, as they would set apart a certain amount as a fund in the name of God whenever they start a business. They also set aside a certain percentage of income as *makamai* (Donation for the temple) for community development. Nagarathars are known for philanthropy and values. Like the Jains' philosophy, Nagarathars also consider business a means of giving back to society through excellent service and discipline. The perspective of looking at business qualitatively, reinvesting profits in business and investing in educational and religious activities make the Nagarathars community renowned for their business acumen and community services at the same time.

Other Business Communities of India:

Other than the Gujaratis, Marwaris, and Chettiars, some of the prominent business communities in India are the Parsis, Sindhis, Jains, Punjabis, Pais, Multanis, Boharis, Bunts (Shettys), Reddys, and Nadars. Though they have also been successful in business, it is difficult to enumerate any distinct business traits except to conclude that all these communities possess qualities like having a nose for business and being good at managing money. A point to note is, some of the business traits these groups followed may be diametrically opposed to those of Gujaratis and Marwaris. For instance, it is said that when Narayana Murthy was working in Patni (a Marwari company) and wanted to start their enterprise with a few of his colleagues who were from South India, one of the things they set out was to create an "Un-Marwari" company. It is unclear what they meant by the same, but the main idea was that all decisions were to be taken by a professional collective, not by a *Sethji* (Owner) and his sons as in a Marwari company.

Like other aspects of India, diversity is visible even in business styles. At the same time, beneath this veneer, a standard set of values can be associated with Indian businesses. We will explore these in the coming chapters.

Exploring the Aspects of the Indian Style of Management

> *"Dance to your own music and take some risks in life because it is often the risk taker who changes the course of history and contributes to the well-being of millions of lives."*
>
> *– Mukesh Ambani, Chairman, Reliance Group*

Having examined the history of business management in India through the ages and the different community-based management styles, I will now attempt to paint a single picture of the Indian style of management. This picture comprises various traits or strokes. Some of the traits have also been compared to the Japanese and American ones to understand where we are from a global perspective.

In the next few sub-chapters, we will discuss the traits associated with the Indian management style in detail. I have also attempted to explain these traits with examples where possible.

Chapter 5A

Business is a Family

"There's a saying in India that goes, 'In a business, treat everyone like family, and they will perform beyond expectations.' This is because, in India, family is everything. And when you treat your employees like family, you build a sense of loyalty, trust, and commitment that is hard to find anywhere else."

– Indra Nooyi, Former CEO of PepsiCo

The history of Indian enterprise is accentuated by family-owned businesses, as in countries like America, Germany, Japan, and others. The family business is a tradition that goes back a few hundred years, if not longer, in India. It is probably apt to say that family businesses are as old as families. Statistics indicate that almost 85% of India Inc. is family-owned. Large corporate business houses like TATA, Reliance, Godrej, Bajaj, Hinduja, Ruia, Thapar, Adani, Birla, Jindal, Mahindra, TVS, Chettinad group and many more are still controlled by the respective families, where the role of the family patriarch is vital and respected. The concept of family businesses in India is more than just with the big corporates. Family-owned entities play a significant role even in micro, small and medium enterprises. Family-owned businesses are estimated to contribute 70% of India's GDP.

Because of this legacy, even today, for most Indian companies, business is like a family. The value system of a family gets organically extended to the business. Similar to how in a family structure, there is an elderly patriarch whom all members respect and abide by, in most Indian companies, the Chairman or the head of the company is like a patriarch who is respected and revered. So much so that the next generation does not want to make disruptive decisions regarding the business as long as the patriarch is alive, preferring to carry out the changes only after the head passes away.

Another aspect of running the business as a family is to put a premium on trust and loyalty over competence when hiring key people. In most family-owned businesses, even today, it is a prevalent practice to place family members in key positions, particularly in financial management. Also, the leadership gets automatically passed on to the next generation based on age-wise seniority. Now, this aspect is also one of the main reasons for feuds in family-owned businesses because of which companies have vertically split. One prime example in recent memory is the Reliance group, which, after the demise of its founder Dhirubhai Ambani, got divided among his two sons – Mukesh Ambani and Anil Ambani in what was a bitter corporate battle that played out in the media for months together before a truce was brokered with the blessings of their mother in true Indian tradition. On the other hand, there are instances where the split has happened more amicably, and the splintered groups continue to thrive and grow. For instance, the Godrej group is going through a split without any public acrimony.

When business is like a family, the employees are like family members. The promoters of the business invariably participate in the good and bad events of the employees. It is widespread for the promoter to extend financial support to the team members who may be at the bottom of the hierarchy for important family events like marriages or deaths. The promoters also make it a point to participate in the staff's family functions. This, I am talking about small and medium companies and not necessarily the large family-owned corporate houses where it is limited to their immediate circle of subordinates.

Hindu festivals, which are part and parcel of Indian culture, are observed and celebrated even in companies with enthusiasm. In Gujarati and Marwari companies, *Lakshmi Puja* is diligently celebrated yearly during *Diwali* where even families sometimes participate. Similarly, in Tamil Nadu, *Ayutha Pooja* is celebrated yearly on the last day of the *Navaratri* festival in offices and factories with gusto. In Kerala, *Onam* is usually celebrated in companies with families of the staff enjoying cultural programmes and traditional *Onam Sadya* (feast).

Due to this inherent nature of treating businesses as families, firing employees doesn't come easily for Indian companies. Unlike in the American business scene, "Hire-and-Fire" does not happen in India even when companies face headwinds in business due to the economy, external conditions or their internal situation. Indian companies would instead go after reduction of expenses like Advertising & Marketing, promotions, training, travel, meeting and conferences before really thinking about retrenchment of employees which is usually taken up as a last resort. Even when retrenchment had to be exercised, the top management does its best to place the affected people in other companies in their network by using their relationships. Employees are seldom left high and dry, like in American companies, without notice. Therefore, for Indians in general, the concept of layoff, which is practised by multinational corporations very commonly, is traumatic and sticks as a social stigma. A point to note is that unlike in American companies where the wage structure is high and, therefore, the wage bill is a significant percentage of an organisation's expenses, the wages are relatively lower in India. Thus, companies prioritise other expense heads in bad times.

Even during the Covid pandemic in 2020, which almost went on for two years, family-owned Indian companies persisted with their employees even when their businesses had nearly come to a standstill during months of a nationwide lockdown. Of course, temporary employees and those with "off role" status were let go, but by and large, those in the organised sector with regular employment in Indian companies were not laid off. Apart from retaining the staff, I am aware of some companies that also took care of the medical and hospital needs of the family members when the entire country was hit during the second wave of the pandemic.

Another example I can quote is of Infosys. It is well-known in the industry that during the dotcom bust of 2001, the board of directors of Infosys decided to take the highest pay cut, followed by a next large pay cut by the Executive Vice Presidents while honouring all offers that were made to fresh graduates. These examples exemplify the compassionate aspect of Indian management of putting the interests of employees before that of their business during a period of crisis like Covid where the employees had no role to play in precipitating the crisis.

When we say that Indian companies treat their businesses like families, I would like to add that the definition of family also extends to the larger community. For instance, in Parsi-owned companies like the Tatas or Godrej, people from the Parsi community are accommodated and given jobs. This is a part of the community welfare measures by which Parsi companies take care of their community's people. This is true for companies in a few other Indian communities as well.

From a strictly business standpoint, treating business as one's family could have fallacies, like not being utterly meritocratic about hiring or promoting people, not being cost-conscious when facing headwinds, and not adopting an utterly professional approach to making business decisions. However, most Indian family-owned businesses still follow the "business is family" mantra and can derive advantages from this approach, the most important one being, the undiluted loyalty of employees who stick with the company through its ups and downs.

In an article co-written by Harsha Mariwala, Chairman of Marico Industries, and Tatwamasi Dixit, they say that the essence of family businesses is their ability to strike a balance between family and business needs, and I agree. Indian businesses, I guess, follow capitalism with a prefix: Compassionate!

Chapter 5B

In Relationships, We Trust

"For me, relationship is significant. I can lose money, not relationships!"

– Sunil Mittal, Founder and Chairman of Bharti Enterprises

Among all aspects of Indian management, if I had to pick the most important one, it would be this. For Indian businesses, more than anything else, relationships matter. While those from India or those who understand the South Asian culture can appreciate this, I find that most others are not in a position to comprehend the significance of building and nurturing relationships while doing business in India. Therefore, this chapter can be considered exclusively for those unfamiliar with Indian culture or ways of doing business. This chapter will also carry a few tips that may come in handy to build relationships in India.

As we saw in the previous chapter, family values are a cornerstone for Indian businesses. In families, trusting each other becomes paramount. Therefore, this gets extended to other stakeholders as well while doing business. Trust cannot be built instantly; it is built over some time. Trust-building follows relationship-building. Once this trust is built, you will find Indian businesses the easiest to work with, in the world. On the other hand, if the element of trust is broken, it isn't easy to continue doing smooth business. More often than not, the relationship ends. This aspect is crucial to understand for managers of foreign companies while dealing with Indian companies as suppliers, customers, or joint venture partners.

So, apart from building trust over time, which is paramount, how do you build a relationship with Indian business people?

- Indians love their culture. A quick study of the culture and a basic understanding of the same does help to break the ice. Being sensitive to the cultural aspects of Indians is the first step. For example, in India, festivals are observed as per the Hindu Calendar, and therefore, they don't fall on the same day of the year every year, unlike Christmas, which falls on the 25th of December every year. Also, not all Indians observe the same festivals. So, from a business perspective, festival holidays differ across the country. Different branches of the same company have different holiday lists in India. In my personal experience, I have seen some expat managers not able to understand this and feeling odd about the same. This is just one example. It is, therefore, essential to understand the culture first and the cultural differences within India and be sensitive towards the same.

- Indians also like talking about different aspects of culture. So, asking questions and clearing doubts help. One must also be prepared to hear other answers to the same question on culture when posed to different people in India because as quoted before, in India, for anything that is true, the opposite could also be true.

- Part and parcel of Indian culture are the Indian festivals, and there are quite a few that happen throughout the year. If you are based in India as an expat or if you happen to visit India during these festivals, it is a good idea to participate in some of these festivals wholeheartedly. *Holi* is a festival of colours that is very popular in the West and North parts of India, during which people play with colours and get smeared with them. Even though drenching oneself with coloured water may not be a comfortable feeling, an expat manager doing just that to celebrate *Holi* – the festival of colours with team members and families goes a long way to building bridges. *Diwali* is another festival that is celebrated all over India with great zeal and enthusiasm and in different ways depending on the region.

- If there is one thing that unifies all Indians wherever you go, it is Cricket. Indians are passionate about Cricket, though it is not India's National sport. Almost all Indians, particularly men, are Cricket experts and can wax eloquently on the game. Except for foreign managers who come from England or its erstwhile colonies, others do not have a very good understanding of Cricket. Therefore, picking up some knowledge of the game if you are working in India is a good idea so that you can engage in meaningful conversation with Indians, particularly during meetings that happen after key Cricket matches. A few months ago, when India lost the finals in the 2023 ICC World Cup for One Day matches, the whole of India was crestfallen. The following week, I attended a business meeting where the key participant was an Englishman. He started the meeting with a few words of comfort for India not winning, though it was the favourite. This broke the ice straight away, and I could see the meeting proceeding very cordially.

- Indians like dancing. Different nationalities adopt different stress-busting techniques. For Indians, dancing and letting their hair down is one way of stress busting. Dinner parties invariably end with dancing. If you are an expat, joining the locals in dancing is a great way to build relationships. During these dancing sessions, which usually follow drinking sessions, Indians are more open to discussing business and non-business matters. I have seen first-hand how expat managers who actively engage in dancing and partying with Indians are welcomed wholeheartedly versus those who prefer to stay quiet during dinners and parties.

- Picking up a few words and sentences in the local language is another tip. I think this may not be a game-changer, but it helps. Particularly in meetings with factory staff and critical company events, throwing some words or sentences in the local language, say Hindi, draws a lot of appreciation. If the expat learns the local language, he also stands to gain a lot of respect. The Managing Director of the Japanese company I worked with, a Japanese expat, landed for a partners' meeting in an auto rickshaw and opened his welcome address with a big *Namaste!* This conveyed the message that the company has imbibed the Indian way! Symbolism works in India!

- While it is not directly related to building relationships since it is connected with culture and doing business, I would like to talk about this – which is the dress code. Indians, by nature, are not naturally inclined to the Western dress code of wearing ties and suits. Though you will find people in suits, jackets, and blazers in India due to business etiquette, it is not an organic phenomenon in India. Indians like to dress in smart business casuals like the Americans. So, if you are an expat, appearing in meetings in simple business casuals will also put your Indian counterparts at ease. In a lighter vein, I would like to share a correspondence between an Indian CEO and his British counterpart visiting India for a meeting. This correspondence is happening through e-mail while discussing the agenda for the meeting and so on. You can imagine for yourself how the issue of relationship-building would have taken shape after an exchange like this:

> Indian CEO: *"So, since we know each other well and we have impressed each other enough, I think we can stick to simple business attire for the meeting and avoid Ties, Suits, etc."*

> British CEO: *"Oh, that's fine. I am not a big fan of Ties and Suits myself, and these days, I wear them only while attending marriages and funerals!"*

- While meetings with Indian counterparts will have a pre-decided fixed agenda, meetings always start with discussing general issues like weather, travel, experience in India, politics, etc. Sometimes, this small talk can extend to a long talk as well. This is used as an icebreaker and also to assess others. So, in meetings, please be prepared to start with small talk. Jumping straight to the agenda or business matter may be construed as being rude.

To summarise, relationships are crucial while doing business in India, so much so that I have seen business tie-ups being called off when people in the scene change and the new people cannot carry forward the legacy of established relationships. This could be a negative point while doing business in India, where business relationships hinge upon individuals involved and not processes and companies. But then, that is the reality in India, and it is essential to be sensitive to it. As someone said, Indians make decisions based on data, statistics, and business cases as much as trust. So, being mindful of building a good working relationship matters while doing business in India. Our *Soch is Nayi, par Rishta Wohi*! (Our thinking is new, but relationships are old).

Chapter 5C

Business is for the Long Term

"Indian management is characterised by a long-term perspective, a focus on collective goals, and a high degree of adaptability."

– Vineet Nayyar, former CEO of HCL Technologies

In India, for time immemorial, the outlook for businesses has always been long term. If you look at some big family-owned corporate houses like the Tatas, Birlas, Godrejs, and Khaitans, they have all been for many decades. It is not difficult to understand the reasoning for the same. Since most of these businesses have large stakes owned by the founding families, the management baton gets passed on from generation to generation. Now, this also extends to other micro, small and medium enterprises. In India, you will find many of these units that are more than 40–50 years old.

When businesses are family owned, they are concerned about long-term wealth creation. It is an Indian trait that families would like to leave wealth for the next generations. The objective is to be successful now and for the next few generations. Not just that, families are also concerned about their social status, family reputation, and goodwill. This inherent need ensures that businesses are managed with a sense of responsibility and financial acumen. Therefore, decisions are made with a long-term view rather than a short-term approach for shoring up profits on a quarter-by-quarter basis or propping up short-term valuations. There is a sense of self-discipline, control, and close monitoring, particularly of issues related to cash flow. This ensures that businesses are run on the back of solid foundations.

This is in total contrast to American companies, where decisions are based on quarterly results. American CEOs are often under tremendous pressure to demonstrate some visible action just for the short term, even if it has an unfavourable long-term impact on the business, as we discussed before. The impact of having a long-term perspective on business is manifold:

1. Indian companies do not shy away from making substantial capital investments in R&D or technology where the payback period is longer. A quick scan of the landscape of Indian-owned companies would reveal that many of the successful Indian companies have ventured into areas like Automobiles (Bajaj, Mahindra), Steel (Tata, Jindal), Engineering (Godrej), Infrastructure (Adani, L&T), Cement (Birla), and so on where the capital investments are high and payback periods long.

2. Customers also build a long-term association with such companies because of the trust they have. They feel confident and assured that the companies will not fold up in the short term, leaving them high and dry for support later on. For instance, customers have been buying Godrej Cupboards for generations just for the trust of the Godrej brand. When companies that have been standing tall for a long time launch new products, customers do not have any inhibitions to try the product because they know that these companies will not disappoint them. On the other hand, I have seen customers quite wary of buying products from foreign companies as they are unsure about the long-term availability of support.

3. Companies with a long-term perspective are positioned to attract and retain the best talent in the industry. This is quite obvious, as companies that have been successful for an extended period are perceived as not short-sighted in their approach and, hence, a better place to work.

4. Companies that have a long standing tend to earn a lot of goodwill from the government of the day. This aspect comes in handy in countries like India, where the role of government in the smooth running of the business is still critical. The government often takes the views of such businesses with a long legacy and success, while formulating policies. Therefore, most Indian companies put a lot of effort into sustaining their business in the long term by even taking short-term hits.

5. Lastly, Indian-owned companies have a sense of responsibility to their employees because of the family values they cherish. This sense of responsibility prevents them from making short-term decisions that may impact their employees' lives. They may prefer to endure short-term losses or shocks instead of making tough decisions that may affect their employees' lives.

I want to add here that all the above points are valid and applicable to all traditional Indian family-owned businesses. The Indian entrepreneurs of today have a different outlook toward business. They are more tuned to short life cycles for their businesses and are concerned about timely exits, with the focus being increasing valuations all the time. This is more applicable now for the knowledge-based new economy with tech-driven offerings. Against a traditional view of starting up a business, sustaining it, and growing it for the long term, the present "start-up" view is to quickly scale up, enhance the valuation, exit with a bounty, and move on to the next start-up. The "Serial Entrepreneur" badge is worn with a sense of pride. In this journey of entries and exits, not all need to be profitable. Failed start-ups are par for the course. Here, I can see a convergence of the American way of doing business and the new Indian way of doing business. But unlike Americans who believe that in the long term, we are dead, for Indians, in the long term, we may be dead, but our *atma* (soul) is eternal!

Chapter 5D

Not Sticking to the Knitting

In the seminal book, "In Search of Excellence," authored by Tom Peters and Robert Waterman Jr in 1982, they mention "Stick to the Knitting" as one of the eight mantras for corporations to succeed. According to this mantra, companies should stick to what they are good or excellent at and not diversify into totally different activities. "Stick to the Knitting," which is essentially a Single Business Strategy, is defined as businesses where 95% or more of revenue comes from one line of activity.

There are merits to this approach, which are:

- Running a single business is less risky than expanding into multiple businesses. A new business is said to carry an 80% risk of failure over five years as per research.
- Single businesses have better economies of scale with high volumes and the inherent cost advantage over competition.
- With one business, management and teams can focus their energies and resources 100% by knowing everything about the business, from products to competitors to technology to emerging trends to threats to the industry, and therefore can manage it better.

- Lesser resources are required when a company operates efficiently in one business line.
- Having only one main product or service sends a message to the marketplace that you are an expert in that area and would stay there for the long term. It gives you an advantage over competitors who make that product one among many.

If you look at the traditional large business houses in India, they have all done the opposite. They have not stuck to knitting and have proved successful not just in their core business but also in the new companies they added. The Indian business philosophy goes against the "Stick to the Knitting" principle and reasoning. In fact, most businesses have gained strength by diversifying. In diversification, there are two types – related or adjacent and non-related. For example, when the Reliance group, initially in the textile business, diversified into polythene and petrochemicals, it was adjacent diversification because it was a case of backward integration. When the same Reliance got into Telecom, it was non-related diversification. While adopting diversification strategies, I found that Indian companies do not make this distinction and generally go in for both types.

Take, for example, the business house of Godrej. Its first business was locks. Did they stick to just making locks or remain in associated businesses? The answer is no. In their over 100 years of existence, the group has diversified into completely non-related businesses and has made a mark in most of them. From Office Equipment to Furniture to Security equipment to Fast-Moving Consumer Goods to Machine tools to Forklifts to even fabricating engines for the Indian space programme, Godrej has thrived and excelled thanks to its diversification. The same can be said for the House of Tatas, which is into businesses as diverse as salt and software. The Reliance group started with textiles and is today into extremely diverse businesses, from refining to retail and even owning cricket teams!

The thought process behind diversifying into non-core businesses differs from group to group. But there are some common aspects that can be attributed:

- Indian business owners are highly enterprising and constantly look for growth opportunities. When such opportunities present themselves, they don't shy away from grabbing them. This can be attributed to the enterprising nature of Indian entrepreneurs in general.
- In India, business is all about scale. There is a limitation to scaling up with just one business. Large businesses get easier access to capital (financing from banks and the public), have the propensity to attract better talent and get the opportunity to be visible to the powers that be. So, the natural option is to scale inorganically by venturing into other businesses, the only consideration being the right business opportunity.
- India is a vast and highly diverse country. A country-wide business requires a certain minimum infrastructure across all regions, like warehouses, branch offices, invoicing points, sales teams, and even multiple production sites. When new businesses are added, there is less need to duplicate most of the infrastructure, and the existing infrastructure can be leveraged. This helps to optimise the cost structures significantly and makes the new businesses more competitive.
- Unlike the wisdom postulated by Tom Peters, diversifying into many businesses helps to de-risk the overall business. When one business is affected for some reason, there is a fallback to other businesses that may not be affected by the same conditions. During Covid and the ensuing lockdowns, I know of certain companies whose business came to a standstill. Yet, in no time, they could sense the opportunity to get into businesses that could thrive during

the pandemic, like selling oximeters, oxygen concentrators, N95 masks, etc. This called for quickly identifying global sources for these items, importing them, and then setting up a distribution model to reach the products to retail stores/agencies across the country, which they did.

- Diversification is also done to better utilise physical assets, including real estate, factories, etc. For instance, land procured for a factory to manufacture washing machines is also used to produce refrigerators so that the land and investment can be optimally utilised across more businesses.

- Utilisation of surplus cash is another motivation for Indian companies to diversify. When corporates are flush with funds, they find it fit to invest in new businesses rather than keep it idle in the balance sheet.

- Most Indian businesses are family-run, and having diversified and different businesses makes assigning responsibilities to other family members easier. I must add here that this is more of a convenient side effect of diversifying and not necessarily the lead reason.

There have been cases where Indian companies entered non-core and non-related businesses and failed the original core business. In my research, this is more of an exception than the rule as far as large Indian corporate groups are concerned. While on this, it is pertinent to recall the term "Diworsification" coined by Investment Guru and Author Peter Lynch in his book "One Up Wall Street." The *"process of investing in too many assets with similar correlations results in an averaging effect. It occurs when an investor adds investments to a portfolio in such a way that the risk/return trade-off is worsened."* Extending the same logic to companies, "Diworsification" is when companies go beyond their core competencies and diversify to areas and end up eroding the overall value of the group.

As far as Indian groups are concerned, they have ensured that their diversification strategy doesn't end up becoming "Diworsification", by first getting the right people on board with the core competencies to run the new businesses. If this required even recruiting expat CEOs with a track record of successfully running those businesses, Indian companies have not shied away from doing that. Indian companies have also been open to tying up with foreign companies through joint ventures when the need arose to acquire technology to manufacture products. In short, the approach has been to "Do what it takes" to ensure they win in the new businesses they enter.

In the pre-liberalisation era, before 1991, Indian companies were basically diversifying based on opportunism. Because of severe controls on production capacities and selling avenues like exports, companies looked to diversify into other businesses to scale up. In that era, the companies enjoyed a ring of protection due to controls on domestic and foreign competition. So, it was of minimum risk to get into unrelated businesses. I reckon the original spark for diversification as a default strategy for many Indian groups must have come from this aspect.

Post-1991, however, Indian corporate groups continued to diversify. But this time, it is not for opportunism but with a more strategic intent to gain a first-mover advantage and leverage the same when sectors are gradually opened up to foreign players. Today, we see that most diversification is happening to move up the value chain.

In the present start-up era, start-ups don't shy away from diversifying, sometimes pretty early in the business cycle, if they find an exciting opportunity and have access to funds. An excellent example is Ola, which started as a taxi aggregator app and has now diversified into manufacturing and selling electric bikes. It seems like a logical extension, but in terms of business dynamics, starting up an App and a factory are as different as Apple fruits and Apple phones!

The Indian approach to aggressive diversification is similar to that of Japan and other Far East economies like Korea. In those countries, while some groups are in related businesses, most are in highly diversified businesses. This is in contrast to America, where large companies remain focused and, by and large, "Stick to the Knitting." Just like how India thrives on Unity in Diversity, Indian businesses thrive on "Scale in Diversity"!

Chapter 5E

Flexible Indians

Flexibility is the key to success in a rapidly changing world. Without the ability to adapt, even the strongest companies cannot survive."

– Kiran Majumdar Shaw, Founder, Biocon India

If, on one end, we find the Japanese style of business to be inflexible, we have on the other end the Indian style of doing business where the hallmark is flexibility. Now, what is flexibility in the context of business? Flexibility is the ability to adapt quickly to sudden or drastic changes in the business environment with minimum disruption. Therefore, flexibility needs adaptability, and both these terms are different, though they are interchangeably used often. Adaptability in business is the ability to fit into emerging scenarios with minimum disruption to the ongoing business. A combination of flexibility and adaptability leads to agility, in my opinion. Flexibility and adaptability come naturally to Indian companies; therefore, they tend to be agile.

Indian businesses are flexible because Indians are trained to be flexible in their lives, day in and day out. For Indians, in their general life, flexibility is not a desired trait but an essential one. There is a saying that India thrives in chaos. Doing business in India is akin to driving a car on Indian roads. As a driver, you need to be flexible, adaptable and finally agile to navigate through the Indian traffic, which, more often than not, is chaotic. Let's look at this analogy in detail.

- Indian roads in their best condition may not be even. Potholes or speed breakers may spring up from nowhere. These are akin to uncertain challenges that crop up suddenly. For example, a political party may call for a sudden *bandh* (Total Closure), which, as a business, can affect your essential meetings, transactions, deliveries, and so on. Indian companies always have a Plan B and an SOP to tackle such sudden challenges.

- It is common for "Take Diversion" signboards to appear from nowhere, even on highways in India. There could be some repair work initiated overnight and being carried on throughout the day, which is why this happens. Similarly, in the Indian business scenario, changes in import duty, GST structure, etc., can happen overnight, and the same comes into effect from midnight. This calls for a recalibration of invoicing systems, stock reconciliation of goods bought at old tax and new, and so on. For a Japanese company, a change like this is a significant disruption. But Indian companies and, therefore, Indian managers are used to even more substantial changes. Handling such transitions has been developed into a core competency by Indian managers.

- In addition to these diversion signboards, some small protests or processions may take place, throwing the traffic out of gear. As a driver, this requires quick thinking or, these days, the agility to look at apps for alternate routes, which will also face a surge in traffic. This is like sudden disruptions that occur in business for which we need to have contingency plans. Indian businesses are quick on their feet at this.

- In addition to all these, extreme situations like heavy rains during monsoons lead to flooding on the roads. Because of this, one may have to abandon the vehicle and pursue alternate modes to reach one's destination. In business, similar situations in India call for flexibility and agility to change well-laid-out and thought-through plans at the last minute. These kinds of disruptions though less these days are common in business scenarios as well. We can see that Indian businesses take these disruptions in their stride and move forward without getting bogged down.

- One point to note is that while driving in India is complicated, the risk for fatalities is lower because of the average lower speeds on Indian roads and highways. Similarly, in Indian businesses, the risk for failure is lower due to these challenges as companies learn to thrive in these conditions right from inception.

As a driver in India, one is trained to handle such uncertainties, and therefore, there is the adage that if one can drive in India, one can drive anywhere in the world. Similarly, it is my belief that if one can manage a business in India well, one can manage anywhere worldwide. Being flexible and adaptable in their approach prevents Indian companies from getting overwhelmed by any sudden business situation or challenge.

Today, we live in an absolute VUCA world, which is a world filled with Volatility, Uncertainty, Complexity, and Ambiguity. As per Wikipedia[20], though this acronym was coined as early as 1987 by Warren Bennis and Burt Nanus to describe the general situation, it was only around 2002 that the term gained more use and traction. But I must add that in the last two years, particularly after Covid and now the Ukraine war, the full importance of this term is being understood and appreciated by the global community at large. In such a VUCA world, flexibility is the one virtue that becomes most important. Managing uncertainties and turbulence is the key to survival first and then success.

In a globalised and connected world, no country exists in isolation. This was amply demonstrated during the Covid pandemic. What started as a virus outbreak out of Wuhan in China sometime in January 2021 soon spread from one country to another, and within three months, most parts of the world were inflicted by the virus. Governments had to resort to hard lockdowns to break the chain. This was an unprecedented situation for the world. In such a situation, even well-thought-out plans and strategies are rendered useless. What is then called for, is accepting the situation for what it is, being flexible to change the well-laid-out plans as per the new situation, and executing the latest plans. Even while doing so, being fully aware that these plans may require change.

Similarly, when we were almost at the fag end of Covid in the first quarter of 2022, when business plans were being worked out for a post-pandemic period ahead, who would have thought that the Russia – Ukraine war would break out and pour water on these plans? If Covid and the ensuing lockdowns, threw a set of challenges, the war posed a totally different set of challenges that needed to be tackled. Even if the war ends, and one hopes it ends sooner, businesses must be equipped to survive in a VUCA world. In the book "Flexible Strategies for VUCA Markets" edited by Sanjay Dhir and Sushil, the authors say that, *"In today's world, strategic flexibility in VUCA is essential for business leaders to sustain market advantage and attain a clear vision amid the chaos."*

As far as India is concerned, much before the acronym VUCA came into being, Indians were used to living in a state of volatility and uncertainty due to the nature of life in India. I believe that Indians are blessed with cognitive flexibility, the readiness to switch between mental processes to generate appropriate behavioural responses selectively; therefore, being flexible comes naturally to Indians and Indian busiensses.

The way most Indian companies coped with the changes in the business environment due to liberalisation in 1991 is a great example to demonstrate how Indian companies were flexible to change with the need. I then worked in the Electronic Business Equipment Division of Godrej & Boyce Mfg. Co. Ltd is the flagship company of the family-owned Indian group, Godrej. This unit was into manufacturing Electronic Typewriters and Dot Matrix printers, marketing the same in India, and exporting to a few other countries. As per the new industrial policy announced in 1991, most of the products came under the Open General License category, which meant that you no longer needed licenses and approvals to import foreign goods in most categories. The then Vice President of our division, Mr. Manu Parpia, saw the imminent threat of prominent global brands not hitherto present in India flooding the Indian market like never before. So, he proposed to the Godrej management that we should tie up with some big companies like Hewlett Packard, Canon, Panasonic, Samsung, and so on and start trading/distributing their products in India. Mr. Parpia's rationale was quite simple. Without its own technology for many of the Office Automation and IT peripherals, Godrej cannot manufacture its own products. If Godrej sticks to its philosophy of selling only its manufactured products, the foreign brands will align with someone else and sell in India anyway. Instead of others doing it, why shouldn't Godrej show flexibility, adapt to the changing needs, and start trading in other brands?

This required a strategic shift in philosophy and thinking. Thus far, Godrej was selling only products manufactured by itself, and that too under its own brand name. Showing flexibility and alacrity, the division tweaked its business model to start trading and selling other brands as well because of which our division soon became the largest distributor of IT products in the country. Few other companies who were competitors to Godrej didn't show this flexibility and continued their own brand and had to struggle against global competition and fade into oblivion soon.

Similarly, the appliances division of Godrej tied up with General Electric. It formed a joint venture for the manufacturing and distributing of appliances, and so did Godrej soaps, which tied up with Procter and Gamble to form a joint venture. Within a few years, these joint ventures fell apart due to conflicting visions and aspirations for both partners, which is another matter altogether. Here, it is pertinent to recall the quote of Forbes, who said, *"Adaptability is a willingness to confront or change your ideas and preconceptions. Flexibility is more a willingness to 'meet others halfway' procedurally."* This is precisely what Godrej demonstrated in the immediate wake of liberalisation.

Another example is Bajaj Auto, a company that had the luxury of keeping customers waiting for ten years to get their new scooters, essentially being in a seller's market. In the post-liberalised era, it got into a completely new business with motorcycles by joining hands with Kawasaki. Today, it has developed its indigenous technology and is among the largest manufacturers of two-wheelers in the world. This required recalibrating the whole approach as a family-owned business and becoming more outward-looking.

Before the 1991 reforms, homegrown companies had little competition, and they never felt the need to innovate or go out of their way to delight the customer. A minimum level of customer satisfaction was enough to preserve their market shares. Liberalisation changed all that. Family-owned business houses like Bajaj, Mahindra, Godrej, etc., are examples of how Indian companies re-invented themselves in the face of intense international competition and continued to grow.

While the above is an example of Indian companies showing flexibility in the face of heat and learning to thrive, the other example of them showing flexibility in the face of new opportunity is how some of the traditional brick-and-mortar companies ventured into the business of software and IT services in the late 90s and early 2000s. The opportunity presented itself in the form of the global Y2K problem at the end of the last century, by which software engineers were required all over the world to fix the Y2K problem in all the prevailing computer systems. On the policy side, tax sops provided by the Government of India to Software Technology Parks provided another opportunity. While many new start-ups like Infosys sprang up to tap this dual opportunity, many traditional family-owned groups like Tata, Mahindra, Wipro, and Godrej jumped on the IT Software bandwagon back then. Thus, today's IT behemoths like TCS, Tech Mahindra, and Wipro were born. Again, this demonstrates flexibility and adaptability combined with the risk-taking attitude we discussed earlier to get into a totally new greenfield sector like IT services.

In the context of being flexible, adaptable, and agile, Indian companies have acquired the ability to read tea leaves, wake up, smell the coffee, and read the writings on the wall.

It is also a fact that flexibility comes as a bane in its quest for excellence as far as Indian companies are concerned. At times, we Indians stretch the concept of flexibility so much that it loses any of its benefits. As I have seen, this comes in the way of proper execution. We plan. We execute. However, the execution may not be as per the plan. This leads to mid-course changes in design, delays in completion, cost overruns, quality compromises, inappropriate allocation of resources, shortfalls in achievements against the plan, and eventually, customer dissatisfaction.

Flexibility, therefore, in my opinion, is a double-edged sword that needs to be wielded carefully. While exercising flexibility to be nimble-footed while navigating in a VUCA world is undoubtedly a competitive advantage, exercising reckless flexibility that leads to poor execution is a recipe for disaster. Therefore, I would say that there is a need to be aware of the "Good" flexibility and "Bad" flexibility, just like the "Good Cholesterol" that is needed for our body and the "Bad Cholesterol" that we need to keep watch on. Indians, by and large, go with the flow!

Chapter 5F

Thriving in a Crisis

"In a crisis, leaders must communicate openly and honestly with their stakeholders and work to rebuild trust and confidence."

– Uday Kotak, Founder, former MD and CEO,
Kotak Mahindra Bank

World over businesses are not strangers to crises. Indian businesses too are not an exception. Crises can occur due to internal circumstances (quality problems, labour strife, sudden employee turnover, cash flow issues…) or external (earthquake, currency turmoil, war, Covid-like pandemic…). The ability to stay calm during a crisis and come out with minimum adverse impact differentiates great managers from others. And if you can turn the crisis to your advantage, then it is a bonus.

Managing a crisis deftly is an art and a science. It calls for a combination of soft skills (keeping away emotions, leadership, team management, communication…) and hard skills that depend on the crisis at hand. In my opinion, if you look at the Japanese, they get highly hassled when they meet with a crisis. Japan, being a very organised and disciplined society where everything happens in clockwork precision, even a tiny deviation from normal comes as a surprise to the Japanese. So, when it is a crisis that, by definition, is quite intense, the Japanese tend to get disturbed and get derailed from their course.

The Americans are better compared to the Japanese when faced with a crisis. They don't get completely bogged down as the Japanese. But even for them, if the solutions are not simple to implement and things get complex, they tend to give up. By nature, the patience levels in Americans are lower. Even Americans do not spend too much time and effort in preparing for a crisis. We saw this during the 2008 Global Financial Crisis. Even when it was too evident that sub-prime lending would land the entire financial system into chaos, regulators like the Fed and banks were hoping against hope without taking timely action.

For Indians, on the other hand, crisis management comes very naturally. Indian businesses do not usually get deterred when faced with a crisis. When faced with a crisis, there could be a chaotic approach to putting out the fire, but even then, there is a method to that madness. The skill of working in adversities and navigating through complex situations, which are inherent when a crisis strikes, is abundant among Indians. And that makes Indian businesses more resilient to crises compared to others. I would like to elucidate this in brief with a few examples from an Indian context:

How Tata Motors Managed the Singur Crisis:

Back in 2005/2006, Tata Motors was looking for a suitable site for putting up a factory for its small car. After looking at different options, it narrowed down to West Bengal state, where the then state government, led by the Left Front, came forward to provide all support to the Tatas. In West Bengal, Singur was the final location identified due to land availability, connectivity, and other factors. However, the first step of the project which is the land acquisition, got into rough weather, which the government or the Tatas didn't expect. It was agricultural land, and while most farmers readily agreed to sell off their land for the factory, one particular group protested vehemently against the same. The matter soon came to a boil with violent street protests after the opposition party led by Mamata Banerjee's Trinamool Congress jumped into the fray to back the protesters.

With the protests turning violent and hitting headlines all for the wrong reasons, the land acquisition could not occur, and the project was pushed back by a few years. Soon, the Tata Group started looking at options outside West Bengal. Bengal's loss turned out to be Gujarat's gain, with the Gujarat government led by the then Chief Minister Narendra Modi rolling out a red carpet to the Tatas. By October 2008, the Tatas, under the leadership of the then Chairman Ratan Tata, announced that they would pull the project out of Singur and shift it to Sanand in Gujarat.

For any other company in the world, such a setback or a crisis would have been too much to handle. It was not just a question of shifting the car factory but also accordingly aligning the supplier ecosystem, which is critical for any mass production unit, particularly automobile manufacturing where the "Cluster manufacturing model" is commonly followed. However, in a remarkable crisis management story, Tata Motors built an entirely new plant from scratch within a record time of 14 months, including the supplier base. Though initially built to produce Tata's small car – Nano, today, the plant produces hatchbacks like the Tigor and Tiago, and by 2018, it reached 100% plant utilisation. The fact that Tata Motors could recover from a setback of such magnitude and still launch the small car – Nano with a delay of just a year or so speaks highly of the crisis management skills of not just the Tatas but also the Gujarat government, which supported Tatas in this shift.

The Satyam Crisis:

Satyam Computer Services, headquartered in Hyderabad, was one of India's top IT Software and Services companies. On the 7th of

January 2009, its Chairman Ramalinga Raju, in a shocking revelation, confessed to a corporate fraud to the tune of Rs 7000 Crore (US$1.4 billion then) on account of over-invoicing, among other manipulations. The company's share price crashed to Rs 11.5 from a historic high of Rs 544 just a year ago. The scandal rocked corporate India and was labelled "India's Enron story". The crisis had a huge ripple effect and had the potential to damage India's software industry, which was riding a high. At stake was the future of thousands of employees and their families, the ongoing engagements with clients, primarily global multinational accounts, retail investors, banks, and finally, India's reputation.

In a very swift move and a first, the then Central Government formed an expert panel comprising Deepak Parekh, Chairman HDFC, Kiran Karnik, Chairman Nasscom, and C. Achuthan, a former member of SEBI, to navigate this crisis. This team did a remarkable job, and within a very short period of three months, the team was able to bring things under control. By April 2009, the company was put up for sale through a public auction route, and a 31% stake in Satyam was acquired by Tech Mahindra, a Mahindra Group company that wanted to expand in the software services space. This calmed the nerves of employees, shareholders, and customers, and by July 2009, the company in its new avatar - Mahindra Satyam, could get back on its rails. This is another example that demonstrates the crisis management competency of Indian companies. Here again, the role of the central government needs to be lauded for getting on top of the situation quickly and empowering the expert panel to find a way out of the crisis. That there was no precedence to this kind of crisis makes it all the more commendable.

The Handling of the COVID-19 Crisis by India:

When the history of this century is written, COVID-19, the pandemic that disrupted the world and turned it upside down, will feature prominently. What will also be written prominently about is how different countries, particularly the big ones in the world responded to the crisis. With the wisdom of hindsight, one can now say that for a hugely populous country, India handled the crisis reasonably well and came out relatively unscathed.

Let us look at the sequence of the government's responses to the pandemic as it unfurled:

- The first handful of cases were reported in India on January 30, 2020. More patients, particularly in Kerala, started appearing towards the end of February.

- By 25th March, the Central Government announced a near-complete lockdown. Though this move was later heavily criticised, it was the only way to "break the chain" of the spreading virus. More importantly, it gave the government time to arrange for the needful stuff, such as oxygen meters, masks, gloves, PPE kits, oxygen concentrators, etc.

- Meanwhile, the government actively worked with private players like Serum Institute and Bharat Biotech to develop the vaccine.

- The other exploding issue was handling the economic stress faced by people at large due to the stopping of economic activity. While other developed nations like the United States resorted to monetary support for all its citizens to prop up demand, the Government of India correctly identified the core issue as a supply-side problem first. The underlying rationale was that even if citizens were supported with cash transfers, they wouldn't just spend money on buying stuff in such a crisis, and even avenues for spending were limited due to the lockdowns. So, the government resorted to supporting people experiencing poverty with free food grains across the country and supporting MSMEs with loan support to tide over the crisis with deferred payment plans.

- Even while announcing these support measures, the government adopted a drip approach rather than announcing everything in one shot, as Covid was unravelling with no endgame in sight. The operating phrase for "keeping the powder dry" for fighting the battle in the coming days.

- By January 2021, the vaccination programme was rolled out in phases. The government again bore the cost of vaccination for all those needy. One of the most important outcomes of the vaccination programme is the launch of the CoWin portal by the Government, with which the entire programme could be monitored across the country.

- By the middle of 2021, the country was hit by a more lethal second wave, putting enormous pressure on the existing medical infrastructure. The government had to respond by focusing on making more beds available and, of course, increasing the capacity of oxygen production.

- During this period, while lockdowns were partially dependent upon the state's situation, the Government continued the free ration programme to ensure food availability for people experiencing poverty.

- By Jan 2022, when the third wave hit India with the Omicron variant, the country was more resilient to handle the increased numbers. However, this variant was milder and didn't require hospitalisations.

- While responding to the developing crisis with a "crossing the bridge as it comes" approach through tactical measures, the government also used the crisis to make some strategic moves. The most important aspect of this is the rolling out of the *Atmanirbhar Bharat* programme to make India more self-reliant and thereby reduce dependencies on other countries for critical needs. Expanding coverage of the attractive Production Linked Incentive (PLI) scheme from three sectors to thirteen sectors in November 2021 in the midst of Covid was another strategic response to give momentum to indigenous manufacturing and take advantage of the shift of supply chains from China.

- In doing all this, the government also ensured that the fiscal situation was under control, because of which today, India could stage the most robust recovery among large economies in the world post-Covid. We have seen that in our neighbouring countries like Sri Lanka, Pakistan, and, to some extent, Bangladesh, their economies have been hit hard and are at the doorstep of international lending institutions like the IMF for bail-out packages. Large economies were hit by very high inflation at the beginning of 2023.

- During this crisis, Prime Minister Narendra Modi also regularly communicated with the public, an essential element in deft crisis handling. At no point in time during the entire pandemic period did the government show any kind of panic.

More case studies exemplify the way India handles and manages crises, but the above is a selection that covers the private sector (Tata Motors), government-private sector (Satyam), and government (Covid). Winston Churchill famously said this after World War II, and one can say that Indian businesses follow this adage conscientiously: *"Never let a good crisis go to waste!"*

Chapter 5G

Family Owned, Professionally Managed

"A professionally managed business is the key to success in today's dynamic business environment."

– Kumar Mangalam Birla, Chairman, Aditya Birla Group

In Chapter 5A, we explored how Indians run businesses as a family. The Indian business universe, as we see it, is still dominated by family-owned companies that extend the concept of family to businesses. While this has been the case since its existence, the significant change we have seen since the 80s and 90s is the advent of professional management.

One of the key factors driving this trend is the increasing complexity of the business environment and the need for greater transparency, and accountability. The changes in the regulatory environment have also necessitated the need for subject matter experts. Many Indian family-owned businesses have realised they must bring in outside talent and expertise to help them navigate these challenges and stay competitive.

In the immediate years after Independence, the ambitions of Indian business people were limited to starting a business and running it smoothly. In India, where the predominant philosophy was socialism, the state controlled how much the companies could grow. There were production capacity controls, pricing controls, sales controls, labour controls, and controls on all aspects of an enterprise. The most important competency for running a business successfully then was the skill of managing the environment, which is essentially managing the government to ensure the releases of permits, licenses, and approvals as smoothly as possible. This era was termed the License/Permit/Quota Raj, which stifled the growth of the Indian enterprise. Combined with this was the control of competition, which meant a highly protected environment for Indian businesses that put a lid on innovation, creativity, competitiveness, improvements, productivity and what have you. In such a controlled environment, the business owners could easily manage the business with hand-picked people from their own family and circle, trust being the cornerstone.

In the 80s and 90s, two things happened for the better regarding family-owned businesses. First, the second generation started taking over the reins from the first generation. Second, liberalisation occurred in India in 1991. Both these had a profound impact on the way family-owned businesses were beginning to be managed. Professional management became an important feature. Let us look into both these aspects in detail.

When the second generation started taking over, the difference was that they came with academic and professional qualifications, unlike the first generation in most cases. Take the case of the Reliance group and Ambanis. Dhirubhai Ambani, the founder of the Reliance enterprise, didn't have a formal education. At 17, he went to Aden and started his career in a trading firm. He returned to India after almost nine years and started his own trading company in Bombay, which exported spices from India and imported textile yarn. Soon, with his business acumen, he made a foray into backward integration and set up the first textile mill. The rest is history and well known. In no time, Reliance grew into this behemoth that ventured into petrochemicals, plastics, power generation, and Telecom. Dhirubhai handed over the day-to-day running of his companies to his sons – Mukesh and Anil by the mid-80s but, continued to oversee the group till his death in 2002.

Now, coming to his sons, while Dhirubhai was a self-made man, he ensured that his sons were educated and professionally qualified to run the business after his term. Mukesh has a Chemical Engineering degree and enrolled for an MBA at Stanford University, which he didn't complete. Anil is a science graduate and did his MBA from the Wharton School, University of Pennsylvania. On their return, both sons engaged with the business actively from the shop floor level before they started heading businesses. With their professional background and exposure to the Western world, they changed the face of the company.

The same happened in other large family groups as well. In the Mahindra Group, Anand Mahindra returned to run the family business after equipping himself with an MBA from Harvard. Adi Godrej of the Godrej group did his MBA from MIT Sloan School of Management, Kumar Mangalam Birla got his MBA from the London Business School, Roshini Nadar, daughter of Shiv Nadar of the HCL group did her MBA from the Kellogg School of Management and so on.

Undoubtedly, the education and the exposure they got from outside the shores of India helped to expand their worldview and opened their eyes to global competition as well as global opportunities in their family businesses.

As the second generation took over, it also realised that it is essential for their businesses to be professionally managed lest they will be finished sooner rather than later. The main reason for the same is, unlike their father's generation, India was no longer a protected country in terms of business. Multinational corporations started looking at India seriously because of its immense business potential, being the second most populous market in the world after China. That they can't run their business in a highly competitive environment with just people from the family soon dawned upon the family-run businesses.

Kumar Mangalam Birla mentioned in an interview that one of the first moves he implemented in his group after he took over from his dad was to vet all applications from family members of existing employees and take them in only if they were found capable. In the past, family members of existing employees were automatically given jobs.

Today, many Indian family-owned businesses have professional CEOs, CFOs, and other senior executives with experience managing large organisations. They have also implemented robust corporate governance practices, including independent Boards of Directors, audit committees, and risk management frameworks.

The other reason for getting professionally managed people on board was to manage the diversifications smoothly and run those companies efficiently. As we saw in Chapter 5D, one of the characteristics and strengths of Indian businesses was not to "Stick to the Knitting" and diversify aggressively. A crucial element of this strategy is to have the right people in the right places. When the Reliance group diversified into Retail for the first time in 2006, one of the first executives to be onboarded was Raghu Pillai, who is considered to be a pioneer in organised retail in India. Pillai, who is deceased now, was instrumental in kicking off multiple verticals from Groceries to Lifestyle stores.

It is important to note that transitioning to professional management is not always smooth, and family-owned businesses face unique challenges in doing so. These challenges include resistance from family members who may feel threatened by outside managers, balancing family dynamics with business needs, and ensuring that the business maintains its core values and culture while adopting modern management practices. Nonetheless, many Indian family-owned companies have successfully navigated these challenges and emerged as leaders in their respective industries.

Professionalisation typically involves bringing in external talent to manage the company, creating a competent Board of Directors, establishing transparent governance structures, implementing robust financial controls, and adopting best practices for management and operations.

Of course, many family-owned businesses in India have struggled to professionalise their management. This is often due to resistance from family members who are reluctant to cede control or a lack of understanding about the benefits of professional management. Nevertheless, the trend towards professionalisation is growing in India, and it is expected that more and more family-owned businesses will adopt best practices to stay competitive in the global marketplace.

"Family Owned Professionally Managed" – is the flavour of the day among family-owned businesses today and this model seems to be yielding results looking at the performance of stocks of many such companies.

Chapter 5H

Indians and Decision Making

"The decisions that matter most in life are made in the heart, not the head."

– Ratan Tata

In the earlier chapter on Japanese management style, we saw how the Japanese are meticulous and rigorous in their decision making. This tends to slow down their decision-making process. They tend to be logical and try to build consensus on any issue. On the other hand, we have the American style. The Americans are quick and audacious in decision making. I would say that the Indian style is somewhere in between, and it is tough to box the Indian decision-making style into a particular type.

In all my experience of watching Indians doing business, I have noticed that there are some fundamental principles that Indians follow while making critical decisions:

- Being logical may not be the only criterion for Indians when deciding. But being practical is critical. This means a decision may not be ideal but will be the most pragmatic considering the situation. Though this is not about business, for easy understanding, I would like to quote this example from global Geo-politics to explain this trait further.

In February 2022, Russia went to war with Ukraine. This divided the world into two camps: On one side are the

Western allies led by the US, which is against Russia and is backing Ukraine. On the other side, you have specific countries that are supporting Russia. As far as India is concerned, it acknowledges that this is not the time for war, and governments must resolve their differences through talks, a stand that it believes in and has articulated openly. However, it is not in a position to openly join the Western allies and completely sever its ties with Russia. Since the USSR days, Russia has been a friend of India, and India still depends on Russia for most of its defence equipment and supplies. Over time, it has started phasing over its supply to other countries, but as of today, India's dependence on Russia is still significant. Under the circumstances, India decided to abstain from voting on all the UN resolutions that were brought up to condemn Russia's invasion of Ukraine. The Ukraine war also pushed up the cost of oil globally, which means that for India, which depends on oil imports to meet its energy security, it is a significant escalation on its oil bill that has the potential to throw its fiscal balance completely. To prevent such a situation, India shifted a chunk of its oil purchase to Russia at a steep discount and favourable payment terms. In this situation, as a torch bearer of world peace and a country that doesn't support unilateral military action, ideally, India should have voted against Russia in the UN resolutions. Again, in an ideal world, it should have continued to purchase oil from its usual sources, even if it is at a higher cost. Now, what India did was pragmatic under the circumstances. By abstaining from the voting, it did not support Russia's stand while signalling support to Russia for its long-term relationship. Also, shifting its purchase of oil to Russia at discounted prices ensured the country's fiscal situation was not hampered due to the increase in global oil prices.

Thus, the government ensured that the people of India were detached from the ill effects of the war concerning oil prices. This is a classic example of the typical Indian way of decision making in business, where Indians tend to evaluate the situation from a practical point of view and make a suitable decision.

We could see this in Tata's decision to stop the production of its Nano project when the sales started floundering. Nano was personally a pet project of Ratan Tata, and because of its unique price positioning as a "People's Car", the world was watching it. However, despite several attempts to re-launch the product, Nano's sales failed to take off. Therefore, instead of continuing the same for emotional reasons, Tatas eventually took a call to pull the plug on its production in 2018, 10 years after its high-decibel launch. This is an example of pragmatic decision-making.

- Data is essential, but instinct drives the final decision. Infosys founder Narayana Murthy famously requoted Edward Deming's words, *"In God, we trust. Everybody else brings data to the table."* His quote talks about how data was central to all decision making in his company, Infosys. However, in general, this may not be the same thinking in most Indian companies. Indian managers analyse data carefully, construct scenarios, including war gaming, and eventually make decisions based on instincts. If the management team instinctively feels optimistic about a project, it may finally just go ahead even though a logical analysis on paper would have presented a negative option. This instinct could also be because of the people involved on the other side with whom trust (as I mentioned earlier) would have been developed. This brings me to the next aspect of the Indian decision-making style namely risktaking. Here, I would like to quote the results of a survey[22] conducted by Salesforce, where eight out of ten business leaders in India said that data plays a crucial role in their decision making. However, the same survey revealed that while companies agreed on the importance of data in decision making, there was a disconnect regarding how data was being used in real terms.

- Indian businesses are aggressive and conservative in taking risks. This may sound conflicting at first read. But the fact is that Indians are both aggressive and conservative in taking risks, and this is influenced a lot by geography and ethnic background. In the earlier chapters, when we discussed different regional styles of Indian management, we saw that Gujaratis and Marwaris have an excellent appetite for taking risks in business. Generally, I have noticed that those from the North and West parts of India (this includes Gujaratis, Marwaris, Punjabis, and Sindhis, for example) are pretty aggressive in risk taking.

On the other hand, those from the South and East parts of India are the opposite and are conservative in taking risks. This makes it complicated to generalise regarding this trait, but those who have dealt with businesses in different parts of India would bear me out on this. However, since the business space in India is dominated mainly by Gujaratis, Marwaris, Parsis, and Baniyas in general, we can safely conclude that Indian businesses are essentially aggressive in risk taking. Incidentally, PWC's Global Risk Survey says that 67% of Indian companies are prepared to take risks to open up new opportunities, which is 5% higher than the global average.

- **Fast and Slow in Decision Making:** We saw earlier that the Japanese are pretty slow in decision making, while Americans are the opposite. As far as Indians are concerned, here again, it is a mixed bag. It just goes to emphasise how complicated India is. Regarding the speed of decision making among Indians, this is what I have noticed. If the decision tends to be favourable, the process is pretty quick. If it is not, then the decision-making process is slow. And here's the reason for the same. Indians, by nature, do not want to say "No." So, when they realise that the decision will not be positive, they either buy more and more time or give some excuse or other for not taking the decision. So, my tip to those who are not from India is, if you find that there is a significant delay in decision making from an Indian company while discussing a business proposal, you can more or less be sure that it is not happening and hence, you should move on and start looking at other options. So, to summarise, a delay in decision making means a "No." If it is a "Yes," things will really move fast when dealing with an Indian company.

- **Trust and Relationships Influence Decision Making:** We have discussed in detail in Chapter 5B how Indian businesses value relationships and trust. Trust and relationships are often highly valued in Indian culture, including in the context of business decision making. Many Indians place a strong emphasis on building and maintaining personal relationships with others, and trust is seen as a critical factor in establishing and maintaining these relationships. This emphasis on trust and relationships can manifest in several ways in business settings. For example, it may be common for Indian business people to spend time getting to know potential partners or clients before entering into formal agreements or transactions. Sometimes, decisions may be made based on personal relationships or recommendations from trusted individuals rather than solely on objective measures such as financial data or market analysis. However, it's important to note that this is not always the case and that decision-making styles can vary greatly depending on the individuals and the specific industry or context. While many Indians may value trust and relationships, they are not necessarily the only factors considered when making business decisions. However, it is a fact that mutual trust and relationships eventually play a pivotal role in swinging the decision even if other criteria are not a complete fit.

Since it is in the open domain, I can cite an example from Geo-politics to substantiate this. It is widely believed that Shinzo Abe, the former Prime Minister of Japan, went out of his way to help India because of his excellent relationship with Narendra Modi, India's Prime Minister. Abe and Modi shared a close personal relationship, and Abe was one of the first world leaders to congratulate Modi on his election as India's Prime Minister in 2014. Abe visited India several times during his tenure as Prime Minister, and the two leaders worked to strengthen the strategic partnership between their two countries. Abe was instrumental in promoting Japan's investment in India's infrastructure sector, including developing the Mumbai-Ahmedabad high-speed rail corridor, being built with Japanese assistance. He also supported India's bid for membership in the Nuclear Suppliers Group and advocated for closer cooperation between India, Japan, and the United States in the Indo-Pacific region. It is also said that the germ of the idea for setting up the QUAD group came from Modi and Abe. Overall, Abe's close relationship with Modi helped to deepen the strategic partnership between India and Japan significantly, and his efforts to support India's development and security goals are seen as a significant factor in the success of the India-Japan relationship in recent years. Though India's relationship with Japan continues to be pretty good, it must be mentioned that it peaked in all aspects during Abe's period thanks to mutual personal rapport.

To conclude, in decision making, Indian businesses follow what I call the "PRINT" mantra: Pragmatic, Relationship-driven, Instinctive, Not risk-averse, and Timely.

Chapter 51

Indian Businesses and Ethics

"In the long run, ethics is good business."

– Adi Godrej, Chairman of Godrej Group

Back in 1991, during the final year of my MBA programme, Godrej & Boyce Mfg. Co. Ltd, the flagship company of the Godrej group, was one of the companies participating in the final year placements at our campus. I applied for it and, as part of the hiring process, had to undergo a written test and a group discussion, after which candidates were shortlisted for a personal interview. The topic for the group discussion, which I vividly recall, was "How important is ethics in an organisation?" I took a stance that ethics and values were indeed crucial, and profits at any cost must not be the sole motive for corporations. During the subsequent personal interview, a panellist mentioned that ethical compliance is a non-negotiable subject at Godrej. Therefore, they appreciated the stance I took during the group discussion.

Regarding the attitude of Indian businesses towards ethics, I have this interesting analogy to narrate and I would go back to Indians and driving! Indian companies following ethics is akin to Indians following signals on the road while driving. Let me explain. When the signal is green, we go. When the signal turns amber, we press the accelerator and go. And when the signal turns red, we see if cops are around, and when we don't find any, we go. The bottom line is we keep going as long as we don't get caught. The attitude of most Indian businesses towards ethics is very close to this.

The instinct to find loopholes in the system and exploit the same till we get caught is somehow ingrained in us. For this reason, you will notice that any consumer or trade promotion announcement in India is always accompanied by a long bullet list of "Terms and Conditions" so that every conceivable loophole is thought through and plugged. In the Japanese company I worked with, the Japanese managers found this very strange as back home, for them, it was all simple and straightforward.

There is a big difference between what Indian businesses want to do and end up doing as far as ethics are concerned. Regarding intention, companies would like to follow ethics and be on the right side of the law. But in practice, business considerations take precedence over intentions. This ties into how pragmatism and flexibility are built into business in India. It is generally felt that in India, companies can thrive only if they are ready to bend the rules, grease palms, and be flexible regarding ethics. Following ethical practices is borne out of convenience and not conviction for most Indian companies.

I must admit that on this topic, it is not fair to generalise and paint all Indian companies with the same brush. But we are going by broad trends and for sure there could be exceptions. In a survey[23] on corporate governance and ethics conducted by Ernst and Young in 2017, 78% of respondents admitted that corrupt practices exist while doing business in India. Surprisingly, the regional average for the Asia Pacific region was not significantly different at 63%. 48% of respondents said it is regular for them to bribe officials in India to win contracts. (In the Asia Pacific region, this was 35%). In the same survey, 57% said that their superiors would overlook bribery, corruption and other questionable activity in favour of business growth. One out of four respondents felt that their managers would comply with controls. The report says that inconsistency and ambiguity in encouraging high ethical standards and insufficient understanding of compliance programmes have increasingly led employees to justify unethical behaviour at the workplace. It is evident from the survey results that for Indian companies, growth trumps ethics.

Another survey by Ernst and Young on Fraud and Corruption in 2015 found that 59% of companies surveyed admitted to frequently reporting their financial results as better than they actually are. Approximately 62% felt that manipulated financial statements are acceptable if there is a specific rationale behind them. I have observed that not only India but the South Asia region generally exhibits a similar approach towards ethics and corporate governance.

As Ratan Tata, Chairman Emeritus of the Tata Group, considered one of the most ethical groups in India, once observed, *"If you choose not to participate in unethical practices, you leave a fair amount of business."* In this context, it is essential to mention that Ratan Tata walked the talk when his group chose to refrain from entering the airline business once earlier as they didn't want to be involved in a corrupt deal that was offered. So, it essentially comes down to the individual company's corporate ethical standards.

Ethics represent an organisation and its staff's moral duty towards its customers, suppliers, shareholders, and society at large. They form the foundation of trust and reliability between the company and its stakeholders. Ethics are ingrained within the organisation's DNA through well-documented systems, processes, SOPs (Standard Operating Processes), policies, rules, and guiding principles. This culture starts from the very top and permeates downwards.

Winds of change are sweeping across the business landscape in India regarding stakeholders' awareness, attitudes, and approaches to business ethics.

a. Companies: Over the years, I must admit that as India moves towards becoming an economic superpower and integrates with the world more and more, there is increasing awareness and emphasis on business ethics. Today, we can say that most of the large Indian groups have well-intentioned and documented guiding principles and policies that govern their day-to-day operations. The transition of management in corporations to the second and third generation family members who have all returned after their studies abroad is also a factor in increasing this awareness towards compliance matters. Thanks to liberalisation and globalisation, Indian companies in the past two decades have had more opportunities to work with Multinational companies like the Japanese, who walk the talk regarding compliance and ethics. This has had a rub-off effect on Indian companies, too.

b. Government: In 2016, the Central government of India introduced the Government e-Marketplace (GeM), an online portal for government procurement. The main objectives of this initiative are to improve transparency in procurement, eliminate corruption in government procurement, and increase speed and overall efficiency. This contactless, paperless, and cashless online marketplace eliminated many issues that were there earlier in the manual procurement system. This is just one example.

In the past few years, we have seen more areas where the government has been pushing for digital transformation, thereby eliminating human interface as much as possible. Today, in India, digital transformation is taking place rapidly across many areas of the citizen-government interface. I can, off the cuff, quote the example of the passport renewal process in India, which has become highly streamlined, quick, and clean. Another example is the renewal of driver's licences. The introduction of digital solutions in many citizen services has significantly helped reduce day-to-day corruption and will continue to drive transparency and ease of doing business in India.

c. Consumers: The fact that winds of change are blowing across in terms of consumers' attitudes towards ethics in India is a welcome development. New research from OpenText has revealed that consumers place such value on buying from ethical brands that 94% are willing to pay more if they can be sure a product has been ethically sourced or produced. As per this survey[24] of 6000 Indian respondents, 94% say that they are willing to pay more for a product if they can be sure it has been ethically sourced or produced. Almost two-thirds (65%) are willing to pay a premium of more than 25% for that product, while 35% are happy to pay 50% more. The survey also shows that nearly a third (29%) of Indian consumers would never buy from a brand again if it were accused of working with unethical suppliers. Instead, they would look for an alternative brand that engages in responsible sourcing. While the survey results come as a pleasant surprise, I feel that at the consumer level, the awakening towards ethics is still at a nascent level. With more awareness of this issue, this can only move in one direction.

d. Individuals: In meeting ethical standards, the role of individuals in society is also crucial. Individuals finally build an organisation, and individuals execute any management's vision. Transparency International's ranking shows India's CPI (Corruption Perception Index) improved from 2.7 to 2.9 from 1995 to 2004 to 3.6 after 2005. There is still a long way to go to get near a score of 9, for being considered less corrupt in the league of countries like Canada, Sweden and Switzerland. It is common wisdom that corruption falls as a country's economy grows and moves from a poor country to an emerging country to a developed one. So, we can expect that India's CPI will also improve significantly as the country's economy grows rapidly.

To summarise, I would say that as far as ethics are concerned, for India as a country in general and for Indian companies in particular, the journey at present is a work in progress. We still have a long way to go before we become a Japan in this regard. Having said that, for a long time, I believed that corruption and ethics have a strong correlation to the economic status of a nation. Developed countries tend to be less corrupt, and poorer countries tend to be more corrupt. Having observed and studied India and many other countries, from underdeveloped to developing to developed nations, I now believe that this correlation is only partially true. An economic superpower like America is not free of business corruption. We may not see petty, low-level corruption in that part of the world. But there, we see high-level corporate frauds and scams with much higher stakes, driven mainly by individual greed to create wealth. Corporate insider trading, stock manipulation, conflict of interest pursuits, fraudulent disclosures, or no disclosures are some cases we have recently seen in high profile companies in the US. Corporate fraud cases have also involved Korean and Japanese companies in India. So, attitude towards ethics and compliance has nothing to do with the economic stature of a country or its people.

Coming back to India, as Ashok Garde wrote in his paper on business ethics in India, *"Most businesses in India act ethically most of the time, but it is a fact that most people do not recognise most of the time!"* There is a visible shift towards a new ethical equilibrium, which could augur well for India in the coming decades as it inches towards becoming the 3rd largest economy in the world.

As someone said, *"Ethics are important, but before that, business is important"* – this sums up the current attitude of Indian businesses towards ethics.

Chapter 5J

Innovation in Indian Companies

"Innovation is not an option. It is a necessity for survival in today's fast-changing business environment."

– Anand Mahindra, Chairman of Mahindra Group

If you ask any of the key captains of the Indian industry about the importance of innovation in their businesses, the answer most likely will be along the same lines as the above quote of Anand Mahindra. There is an explicit acknowledgement that innovation is what gives any company the competitive edge required to stay on top or even survive. Yet, if one looks at the ground reality regarding the role of innovation in the growth of Indian companies, it is a mixed bag.

What is innovation, first of all? As per the English dictionary, it is nothing but a novel idea, method, process, or device. In business, however, I like the definition of the author Lisa Caprelli, who says, *"Innovation is using new technology and using new ways of thinking to add value to an existing idea or product or service and to make substantial changes in society."* So, the keywords around which the act of innovation is pivoted are "new," "technology," "idea," and "societal transformation." Innovation must, therefore, lead to creating new economic value.

As a country, we pride ourselves on contributing to the fields of mathematics, astronomy, medicine, wellness, space research, etc.

However, in the last few decades, the result would not be anything to write about, if we put India to the test of Caprelli's definition of innovation, though we have demonstrated ourselves to be an excellent reverse engineering country. This prompted Narayana Murthy, former Chairman and Co-founder of Infosys, to once lament that there is "no earth-shaking idea" that India has given to the world in the last 60 years, and he is probably right. This is even when India boasts of being the world's most significant skilled IT workforce source. Engineers of Indian origin dominate the workforce in most technology companies today in terms of numbers. Indian brains may be behind some of the breakthrough ideas that have come out of Silicon Valley for sure. Yet, no Indian company or enterprise has been at the forefront of such ideas. In this context, people often look up to a country like America, which has been the birthplace of breakthrough ideas like Google, Uber and the iPhone, to mention just a few.

This begs the question as to what it takes for a society to promote innovation. Though this is a complex and multifaceted question, there are some pointers towards answering it. It is said that innovation needs to be in a society's DNA. Does India have it in its DNA? The answer, in all probability, would be no. The reasons are not difficult to explain:

1. System of Education: Innovation comes from thinking, for which an education system that kindles thinking is essential. All stakeholders in India almost universally acknowledge that the Indian education system, with its emphasis on marks, grades, and examinations, promotes, or rather encourages rote learning. It doesn't inspire students to wear their thinking caps at all but rather drives them to memorise and reproduce. The New Education Policy and various reforms in the curriculum and teaching

methods in schools attempt to change this. Over time, we can expect these changes to bear fruit.

2. Hierarchical System: In India, whether at home or in the workplace, we still follow a regimental hierarchical system. This is an antidote to nurturing creativity and original thinking. A survey conducted by CII-ITC pointed out the hierarchical system as a hindrance to promoting innovation in Indian companies. A hierarchical workplace tends to be a hurdle to free thinking and expression, as people always try to be conscious and cautious of expressing their ideas. This applies to a hierarchical society like Japan too, which is not at the forefront of breakthrough ideas. Japan has always excelled in what I call "Incremental innovation", whereby the Japanese are good at taking existing stuff and vastly improving on it. Therefore, a non-hierarchical society like the US is more conducive to innovation, and we can see it for ourselves.

3. Economic Stature of our country: This point will come up when discussing most problems facing India. The economic stature of a country becomes relevant for promoting innovation too, because promoting innovation requires a lot of financial resources. If we are economically a strong country, it becomes easy to allocate funds to, say, research and development, incubator labs, ideas factories, and so on and justify the same. When we are still a developing country with a substantial population still living in poverty, it becomes a question of prioritising one over the other. Therefore, it is natural that our fund allocation towards areas that can foster innovation, whether by the government or private enterprises, is still low. But this is changing, and as India keeps growing at a fast clip as it is today, we can expect this impediment to be bridged.

4. Being a Risk-Averse Society: For innovation to flourish, risks must be taken. Ideas are generated by trial and error

at multiple levels. Playing it safe and following a set path doesn't work. It needs a risk-taking attitude to keep going at it without fear of failure. This plays at two levels. One is at the attitude level where failures are not reprimanded and, on the contrary, empathised with encouragement. Second, at the financial level, there is the capacity to withstand losses, which comes as part of the earlier point on the economic stature. The confidence to take risks comes from the understanding that failures are okay and that financial loss can be managed. Again, I feel that this aspect of India is a work in progress now and can change in the next two decades, if not earlier.

5. Role of the brain: As per the Right brain – Left Brain theory of Nobel Laureate Roger W. Sperry, each side of the brain is associated with different types of thinking. A Left-brained person is said to be more logical, objective, analytical, and practical. This person will likely be clued to facts, numbers, and a structured line of thinking. On the other hand, a Right-Brained individual is likely to be emotional, artistic, freer in her thought process, and hence more creative. Innovation needs more contributions from the right brain to flourish in society. Though no research establishes the percentage of right brainers in India, it is my conjecture, based on what I see around, that India is a land of left-brainers. That's why we have more engineers, doctors, accountants, and scientists and fewer people who are into fine arts and other creative professions. This directly correlates to the innovation-related output that comes out of our country. Subroto Bagchi, Co-Founder of the IT company – Mindtree, says, *"Innovation happens when you intensely love something. But we fail to innovate substantially in India because we only have engineering capacity and not such intense thoughts or feelings towards anything."* When I

was growing up, most of my batch mates, and in particular the toppers, pursued Science or Commerce, and very few opted for liberal arts. So, the passion for creating, love, and feelings all play an essential role in inducing creativity; therefore, the brain plays its part in promoting innovation.

6. Access to Capital: This is where the concept of the start-up ecosystem comes into play. Start-ups, by nature, are more risk-friendly, innovation-driven, and flexible, whose founders wear passion on their sleeves. However, in the past, start-ups in India found it extremely difficult to access capital, particularly in the early stages where sustaining the efforts is critical. In countries like the US, start-ups could tap the ecosystem of venture capitalists and angel investors, backed by sizeable private equity, limited partners (LP), and general partners (GP), in short, large institutional entities. In India, we also have a flourishing Venture Capital ecosystem backed by the government's initiatives. However, this is still a work in progress in India compared to large economies like the US and China. Soon enough, I hope we will get over this, which will have a direct impact on the innovation coming out of India.

7. Lack of Systemic Process for Innovation: More than society, this has more to do with companies that fail to encourage innovation, as it gives results only in the long run with a high probability of failure in the short-term Unless there is a well laid out process for promoting innovation in an organisation that encompasses a well-thought-out strategy, structure, top management's mindshare, resource allocation, training, and continuous review, it is not going to pay off even in the long run. Such a commitment has been missing in most Indian companies, who instead prefer to take the low-hanging fruit route of opting for the well-trodden, beaten path over innovation. Even in the technology and app space, where India has seen the rise

of a variety of successful start-ups, almost all of these are clones of successful products that were innovated in other countries. We are yet to see a top-notch product or an app that can be said to have originated from India.

Having listed all these constraints for promoting innovation, on the positive side, there are a few pointers that augur well for India on the innovation front:

1. The intent and role of top management in India towards fostering innovation have been highly encouraging. A Hays group survey of Top CEOs of publicly listed Indian companies found that Indian CEOs are at the forefront of seeking new ideas, information, and technology to improve their business.

2. Incidentally, India comes out top as the "Best Innovative country" in Central and South Asia as per the Global Innovation Index 2021 ranking. Not just that, in relation to its level of development, it retains its top position as overperforming on innovation for the 11th year in succession.

3. The "India Stack" that is built with Aadhaar (Digital Identification), Interoperable Payments through UPI (United Payments Interface) that can be used with multiple payment wallets, and a paperless verification of digital documents, is creating a revolution in financial inclusion in the country while increasing efficiency and convenience. Though none of these three elements of the India stack are unique, the combined product's power has been exceptional and can be called a game-changing innovation from India. This adoption of public infrastructure has made the delivery of public services more inclusive, efficient, and cost-effective while also allowing private enterprises to leverage the same for the efficient delivery of their products at lower costs.

4. Indian tech companies have now integrated well with the global tech industry. This helps knowledge sharing and learning to widen the exposure of Indians to other highly innovative societies like the US.

5. The demographic dividend India is enjoying now with its pool of highly skilled, young tech workforce can be a prime mover for innovation and growth in the world.

6. India is a highly diverse country with respect to culture, background, race, religion, demographics, and psychographics. With the other factors that help innovation coming into play, diversity helps promote creativity, out-of-the-box thinking, and innovation.

7. India now ranks third in the global start-up ecosystem, which can propel innovation in India on a scale never before seen.

India might not have been known for its contribution to innovation in the past, but the above enabling factors promise a massive transformation in the coming years. Having said that, one area in which India has long been at the forefront is day-to-day innovation, called *Jugaad*. In the next chapter, we will look at the phenomenon called *Jugaad* in detail.

Chapter 5K

India – The Land of *Jugaad*

"Jugaad is not just a hack; it's a way of life."

– Navi Radjou, Co-Author of the book Jugaad Innovation

In colloquial Hindi, *Jugaad* is nothing but a quick fix that doesn't require too many resources and doesn't cost so much money. More importantly, it involves the use of the brain creatively and innovatively. In their regular lives, Indians have been doing *Jugaad* day in and day out from time immemorial. When a problem presents itself, the immediate instinct for an average Indian is how to do *Jugaad* and fix it. Again, to reiterate, the idea is to fix it right then, with whatever resources are available and without spending too much money. Time and resources are also eventually money. So, as author Navi Radjou says, *Jugaad* is not just a hack. It is a way of life for Indians.

A few years back, we moved to a new flat after we completed the woodwork and interiors. We found that the doors of the wooden cupboards, which were fitted with magnets, were very stiff to open. We brought it to the attention of the chief carpenter and asked him to check why it was happening and fix it. What he did to fix this is what I would call a *Jugaad*. He just put strips of transparent cello tape on the magnets, and voila, it became much easier to open the doors now. The fix was quick, cheap and creative. He didn't try to replace the magnets with less magnetic strength etc. Welcome to India, the Land of *Jugaad*.

If I have to trace the origins of *Jugaad*, then it will come back to the simple and frugal lifestyles adopted by Indians over the last century, when the majority of Indians were poor or had low incomes. So, the instinct was to use, repair, reuse, and refuse (to throw).

For example, when I was a kid and my slipper gave way, my parents quickly fixed it with a safety pin and made me use it for a few more days or even months. When it gave way further, an attempt would be made to repair it by the neighbourhood cobbler so that it could be used for a few more weeks. It is only when it gives way finally that a thought of buying a new pair would occur. I am sure this would have been the scenario in all middle-class homes in India in the pre-90s.

Today, the 5R concept in sustainability, which stands for Refuse, Reduce, Reuse, Repurpose, and Recycle, is very much in vogue globally. But in adopting *Jugaad* as a way of life, Indians have followed a set of 5Rs, namely Refuse, Reuse, Repurpose, Recycle, and Repair, for quite some time.

Jugaad in Indian Business:

It is this inherent psyche of Indians that has made *Jugaad* an essential aspect of Indian businesses as well. Whether it is on the shop floor of a factory, a warehouse, or the marketing war room in an Indian company, *Jugaad* is an omnipresent concept when it comes to fixing problems. *"Is there a Jugaad for this?"* is the boss's first question when confronted with a problem. This makes the team rack their brains to develop a quick, less expensive, and creative solution so that the problem can be out of the way once implemented.

In job interviews, while selecting people, particularly for operations, the question – *"Are you a Jugaadu?"* should not come as a surprise. The interviewer seeks to know if you are quick on the feet and brain to fix problems. And this is considered to be a virtue.

Jugaad, which was hitherto a common day-to-day concept, attained corporate status when Jaideep Prabhu, Navi Radjou, and Simon Ahuja wrote a book on it titled "Jugaad Innovation". In a way, the authors, through this book, took this concept out of India to the globe. The book provides examples of how companies worldwide, like Future Group, Renault-Nissan, Meta, Yes Bank, and Tata Group, among others, practice *Jugaad* to innovate and grow. The book presents ways to innovate, be flexible, and do more with less. Now, all these are also inherent traits of the Indian style of management, which is why *Jugaad* naturally fits in as one of the critical characteristics of the Indian management style.

In the book *Jugaad Innovation*, the authors have developed six guiding principles for applying *Jugaad* in business. They are:

"1. Seek opportunity in adversity

2. Do more with less

3. Think and Act flexibly

4. Keep it simple

5. Include the marginalised

6. Follow your heart"

I want to add another guiding principle here: do not be "Penny-wise and pound-foolish" when adopting *Jugaad*.

In Mumbai, where I live, the roads are full of potholes during monsoons and this is an annual feature. These potholes slow down the already slow traffic on Mumbai roads, leading to a massive loss of productivity and increasing the mental stress of the public. Every year, the Municipality does a shoddy job of fixing the potholes amid the monsoons which give way quickly. In what can be classified as *Jugaad*, the Municipality uses a cold patch such as PatchMaster. This does the job for the present but is never a permanent solution. What is required here is a more permanent solution than a quick fix that saves money in the short term.

One of Infosys's co-founders, Nandan Nilekani, once said that *Jugaad* results from a dysfunctional system. While *Jugaad* represents frugality, ingenuity, and minimalism to some, others feel that the word denotes a quick, immediate fix that will eventually have long-term repercussions.

In this context, I must say that *Jugaad* as a concept is the antithesis of the Japanese thinking style. In Japan, solutions to problems must be thought through and need to be perfect for the long term, even if they cost more. In the Indian way of thinking, a quick fix that is cheaper and works for the short term is acceptable as long as the work gets done for the time being.

Here's where the concept of *Jugaad* being interlinked with the economic status of a society comes into the picture. *Jugaad* is not seen as a virtue in a developed country like Japan, while in a developing country like India, *Jugaad* becomes essential and relevant. Again, I think that as a country grows economically, its *Jugaad* instincts would wane. These days, we practice less *Jugaad* at home. Equipped with more disposable income due to the growing economy, our urge to seek quick, cheap fixes has been reduced. Along with it, what is reduced is the ability to use the brain for that purpose. Our *Jugaad* instincts are weaker than our parents, and I am sure our children's *Jugaad* instincts will be weaker than ours as we continue to grow.

There is also an increasingly visible commentary that the celebration of *Jugaad* is killing real innovation in India. It is felt that *Jugaad* promotes a *Chalta Hai* (easy-going) and *Kaam Chalau* (Manage with whatever) attitude, which goes against its very founding principles. From being asked *"Are you a Jugaadu?"* in a venerable way to being told *"Don't be a Jugaadu"* in a chastising way, *Jugaad* has seen a 180-degree shift in its acceptance.

Does that mean the days of *Jugaad* in India are numbered? I don't think so. Our thinking style, whether at home or work, will continue to be *Jugaad*-oriented. But we will only be left with the "Good *Jugaad*," which are genuine hacks to problems in line with the original definition of *Jugaad*. The "Bad *Jugaad*," which is more of a lazy hack that fixes the problem in the short run while creating problems in the long run, may cease to prosper as our economic status grows.

It is essential, however, for businesses to continue to seek innovative solutions for their problems through "Good *Jugaad*," which could be in the areas of Operations (Logistics/Supply Chain/Customer Service), marketing, design, and product development. When the concept of *Jugaad* is practised well in businesses like Indians do, it has the following benefits:

- Brings down the cost of Operation, which is quite obvious
- Saves time, which is again cost savings
- Facilitates entry into new products/segments with innovative design
- Corporate Social Responsibility
- Promotes sustainability
- Improve profitability overall.

Jugaad is here to stay for Indian businesses, and it will remain a unique export from India to the world. Any definition of the Indian management style cannot be complete without including the concept of *Jugaad*.

Chapter 5L

Indian Marketing

It isn't easy to convey the criticality of marketing in business better than how marketing Guru Philip Kotler has put it in the above quote. In addition to innovation, Marketing is one function that can make or break a business forever. It is interesting to see how various countries have fared over the years regarding marketing prowess.

If you look at the large economies, the one country that has been a trailblazer and a leader in the world in the domain of marketing is America. America and the Americans know their marketing very well. No wonder we have seen a deluge of brands born in America that have gone on to become successful not just in America but all over the world. This is not just restricted to one product category; American brands have made an imprint cutting across multiple categories from Coke and Pepsi in Beverages to McDonald's and Pizza Hut in Fast Food to Ford and GM in Automobiles to GE and Whirlpool in Appliances to Dell and HP in Computers to Google and Apple in Tech and so on. Even as a tourist country, America has marketed itself well with its Hollywood and Disney land products, which other countries have tried to emulate, often with mixed results.

On the other hand, I would say Japan is a country that is not revered for marketing so much. In the era after World War, when

Japan started designing, manufacturing products and exporting them to other countries, they focused on providing better quality and better-featured products at a lower price than existing competition. It was only much later that Japanese companies started talking about their superior quality and user-friendliness and selling them at a premium price. Yet, they could not build a brand recall like American brands in other parts of the world for a long time. It was only much later that Japanese companies realised this shortcoming and started focusing on marketing and brand building, which is why we can see iconic brands like Sony, Panasonic, Toyota, Nissan, etc. Even here, Japanese brands are more in the consumer durables and auto space and are not spread like the American brands. In marketing, the Japanese have only followed the footsteps of Americans. Regarding priority, marketing comes somewhere down the ladder as far as Japanese companies are concerned.

Now, coming to India, I would say that we are somewhere in between as far as marketing is concerned. But we are certainly better at marketing than some larger economies like China. Our marketing instincts have been poor as a country, borne out by the fact that many of our strengths are unknown to the world because we have not bothered to market them well.

Even concerning tourism, India offers a diversified portfolio of places from hill stations to beaches, historical landmarks, spiritual destinations, adventure sites, and shopping, catering to a wide range of interests of domestic and international tourists. Yet, for various reasons, one being lackadaisical marketing, India ranks very low as a tourist destination, with a smaller country like Thailand attracting roughly four times the number of foreign tourists than India (Reference: Year 2019 – Pre-Covid year).

Only in the past few decades have we started taking marketing seriously as a country. For Indian homegrown companies, many marketing concepts and practices have been passed down the line by foreign companies (mostly American) when they were associated in some form or other.

In the period after Independence and till the 1990s, the Indian companies operated in a sellers' market rather than a buyers' market, with limited choices for the Indian consumer in most categories. Therefore, the marketing required in that environment was minimalistic and needed just about to maintain market positions among limited players. Ironically, any attempt to fuel demand with innovative and aggressive marketing would meet supply constraints.

Yet, in that controlled environment, a few Indian companies did market their products well and successfully built many *desi* brands, which became extremely popular in India. The 70s and 80s were a golden period for Indian homegrown brands, with the advent of Colour Television in 1982 in India. One of the critical aspects of marketing is, of course, advertising. Till then, advertising was limited to Print, Radio, Billboards, Handbills, Commercials in Cinema Halls, and so on, and therefore, its reach was directly related to literacy levels in India. However, the advent of TV in India made mass advertising possible. With that, there was an explosion of brands in India and the impact of marketing with demand growing in not just the metros but expanding to smaller towns. I can think of homegrown brands like Rasna, Nirma, BPL, Videocon, Ceasefire, Thumsup, Wipro, HCL, Amul, Vimal, and Godrej, to name a few, getting a top-of-the-mind recall in their respective categories.

The post-liberalisation phase after the 90s is when Indian companies and, therefore, Indian brands started feeling the heat of competition in the real sense. Competition came not just from global brands but also from other Indian brands that started dreaming big. With the removal of controls on production capacity, imports, foreign exchange, and foreign collaborations, Indian companies could think big of expanding both within India and overseas. This is the phase in which Indian companies understood real marketing for the ensuing reasons.

With the advent of foreign competition, they could see what foreign brands were doing in marketing to establish their brands in India. The lessons were threefold. One is where foreign companies followed established marketing ideas and made them successful in India (Example: Pepsi, Coke, HP, Samsung, etc.). Two, where foreign companies took the fundamental marketing concepts but customised them to suit Indian culture, tastes, consumer preferences, and economics. (McDonald's, LG, Philips, Hyundai, etc). Third, where foreign companies introduced the same global marketing ideas but failed as they didn't resonate with the Indian consumer (Kellogg's, Ford, etc.)

1. With the economy opening up, many Indian corporations got the opportunity to tie up with global majors. These associations helped Indian companies learn best practices and processes in many areas, including marketing. For example, Godrej Soaps was an established Indian company with homegrown soap brands in India. In 1991/92, it entered into a joint venture with Procter and Gamble (P&G). Though the joint venture didn't survive for long, the Indian arm could get exposure to how the American company worked, particularly in the area of marketing, where P&G was powerful worldwide. America being a trailblazer in marketing, Indian companies that had a tie-up with American companies could imbibe many marketing concepts and practices from the American companies.

2. In this phase, the second generation of family-owned businesses in India was also returning to India after their studies abroad. Since most of them had been to the US for

their studies, they were exposed to many American brands and their marketing methods. When they returned, they talked about those practices to the Indian managers, who willingly implemented them.

3. With the opening up of the media, particularly television and, later, the internet, it was easy to look at best practices in global marketing and brand building. This made a significant difference in Indians' gaining knowledge and insights, which can be seen in the marketing and brand-building approach of Indian brands from the beginning of this century.

4. With the above changes, many new Indian brands could come to the limelight and spread their wings outside India. On the other hand, some of the popular brands of the pre-90s era (BPL, Videocon, and Rasna, for example) soon faded away. It is not just because of marketing that these brands failed; they couldn't stand up to competition from new domestic and global players.

It was in this period post-2000 that we saw many Indian brands going global with their ambitions and becoming successful. If you have to look at Indian brands that have made an international impact, they can be counted on your fingers. Some of the "Made in India" brands with a global recall that come to my mind are Tata, Infosys, Taj Mahal, Taj Hotels, IPL, Wipro, Maruti, Bajaj, Hero, Asian Paints, Airtel and Fevicol. But beyond products, some generic categories have originated from India and become hi-recall brands like *Yoga*, Butter Chicken, Basmati, Turmeric, *Jugaad*, etc. Even here, in some cases like *Yoga*, which today can be touted as a *desi* brand that has a global recall, the product has existed for centuries, but it is just now that we have managed to put it on the global map.

Turmeric has been part of our kitchens and cuisine for centuries. From one generation to another, we have been told that turmeric has rich medicinal properties. *Haldi*, which is how turmeric is known in India, is part of everyday food in India. In Ayurveda, turmeric is believed to have medicinal attributes like relieving gas, dispelling worms, and improving digestion, among other benefits. *Haldi ka Dudh* (Hot Milk with Turmeric) is often a grandma's remedy for throat irritation or infection. Turmeric also is supposed to be a disinfectant and good for the skin. Women have used turmeric paste for years. In North India, during marriages, a *Haldi* ceremony takes place a few days before the wedding at the bride and groom's home, where freshly ground *Haldi* paste is applied to the bride and the groom's body, including face, legs, hands and neck. *Haldi* is believed to have cleansing properties as per Hindu custom. While all this about *Haldi* is known and therefore has been used extensively in India, it is only now that the world is aware of it. On a visit to Starbucks in the US a few years ago, I was pleasantly surprised to see our own *Haldi Ka Dudh* being offered as "Turmeric Latte" on the menu. Just this addition will strengthen the brand *Haldi* or Turmeric more than all our efforts to popularise *Haldi* in India till now!

Having said that, Indian companies have woken up to reality and are pursuing marketing with all seriousness in the last couple of decades. There is a clear awakening that, at the end of the day, brand value plays an essential part in enterprise value. Even in the government sector, a very successful case study for marketing is Kerala Tourism with its "God's Own Country" positioning. It is a classic case of how a tagline for Kerala Tourism with some brilliant marketing has become the state's positioning for everything over the years. Similarly, we saw how the Central government had made a success out of many of its initiatives through smart marketing efforts. Initiatives like "Make in India", *Atma Nirbhar Bharat, Swachh Bharat* and so on have attained traction due to some great marketing efforts. As an aside, I would like to add that Barack Obama's Presidential campaign in 2008 is hailed as among the best in political marketing in the world. Taking a leaf out of the same, which was predominantly social media and internet-driven, Narendra Modi ran his Prime Ministerial Campaign in 2014 as a 360-degree campaign covering traditional media (print, TV, outdoor), social media and on-the-ground activation through carefully choreographed events like *Chai Pe Charcha*. Later on, Modi's campaign in 2019, which followed up on the *Abki Baar* theme with the slogan – *Phir Ek Baar, Modi Sarkar*, was so successful and popular that David Cameron customised the same as *Phir Ek Baar Cameron Sarkar* during the UK elections to woo the Indian community.

With the media landscape moving from traditional media to digital/online media, India, with its inherent strength in IT and tech, has also been at the forefront of this marketing transformation. Indian companies have quickly taken into digital marketing and social media marketing. The combination of India's strength in the English language and software has helped Indian companies quickly adopt digital marketing techniques. This is not just limited to large Indian corporations but also small and medium businesses, micro-businesses, and start-ups. Since online marketing doesn't have the constraint of geographical boundaries, Indian companies could transcend the physical boundaries of India in terms of branding and become global brands more easily than before. Paytm, a payment wallet launched in 2010, became popular in 2016 after Demonetisation. Since then, Paytm, while being the leading E-Wallet in India, has expanded to other countries like Japan, Canada and even the United States. There are other examples of new brands like Ola, a ride-hailing app like Uber that has become popular in India and expanded overseas with high brand recall.

One of the aspects of marketing where Indian companies and brands have constantly displayed a high quality of output is "Brand Activation." Brand Activation is a tool by which a brand engages with the consumer directly to promote a personalised experience.

The user gets an opportunity to see, touch, feel, and use the brand and get a first-hand experience. India has been the birthplace of many pioneering ideas in brand activation. One of the most creative, innovative and effective brand activation ideas was the one done by the Indian subsidiary of Unilever during the *Kumbh Mela* festival at Allahabad (now Prayagraj) in 2013. The *Kumbh Mela* is the largest human congregation on the planet. At the Kumbh, Lifebuoy, which is a soap and hand sanitiser brand, as part of its brand activation campaign, arranged to supply *rotis* that were heat stamped with the message *Lifebuoy se haath dhoye kya'* (Have you washed your hand with Lifebuoy?). The campaign ran for 30 days, during which 100 promoters worked in 100 over kitchens and stamped over 2.5 million fresh *rotis*. The campaign reportedly cost about Rs 2 million (US$36000) and directly reached over 5 million people there. In addition, thanks to its innovation, the campaign got a huge PR boost worldwide and became a global case study for brand activation.

While on this, I also want to talk about specific campaigns that Indian subsidiaries of multinational companies carried out that became successful in India and were then adapted to other countries. For example, in 2013, Pepsi launched the "Oh Yes *Abhi*" campaign in India to target the youth as always. The basic theme of the campaign was "living in the moment" and featured Bollywood celebrities. The campaign was highly successful in India and was later adapted to markets like Africa and the Middle East.

"Kuch Meetha Ho Jaye" was another campaign that was conceived in India by Cadbury's and launched in 2007 to promote its chocolates as a "good news/happy event/joyous moment" need. This campaign featured Amitabh Bachchan and became a massive success in India. This campaign was then adapted and used in the United Kingdom and South Africa.

The above case studies point out that marketing in India is a far cry from the '60s and '70s when ideas from the West were copied and pasted with minor variations. These days, India is also the birthplace of some incredible marketing ideas that have been adapted and used in other markets globally. Marketing and Advertising professionals from India are now routinely given responsibilities for regions outside of India as well.

In conclusion, though India is not a country that is inherently strong in marketing or has marketing in its DNA, it has come a long way in this field. Marketing may not be our forte, but we are getting there. The long-standing gap between India and America, the pioneer and leader in marketing, has narrowed considerably recently. This progression in the right direction as far as marketing is concerned will bode well for the future of Indian companies that have ambitions to be leaders not just in India but also in global markets for indigenous products and services. If Kerala can become "God's Own Country", India can be "God's Own World" with some marketing!

Chapter 5M

The Indian Manager

"Indian managers have a unique ability to balance the demands of traditional hierarchies with the needs of a rapidly changing landscape!"

– Ravi Venkatesan, Former Chairman, Microsoft India

Any commentary on the Indian management style will be incomplete if we don't include the facets of an Indian manager. After all, Indian management is nothing but a reflection of the collective consciousness of Indian managers. Homegrown *desi* managers, like managers of other nationalities, come as a package of positives and shortcomings. These directly reflect the aspects of Indian management we covered in the past chapters.

As we have discussed before, India is not a homogeneous country. Even among managers, you will find the most diversified talent in the country, where the traits change from one region to another. This is a favourite real-life story I share often based on what I have seen in different companies I have been associated with in my career. In All India sales team conferences, you will find different regions behaving differently. The team from the North will be the most vocal during the meets and boisterous during the parties. The South team will be very measured in their interactions and mostly talk among themselves during the meetings but are noisy at the evening parties. The team from the West will be balanced in their interactions during the meet and off-meet hours. The

East team will be quiet all the time. This is very typical in India, I would say.

The set of traits we are attributing here to the Indian managers is not region-specific but more generalised.

Indian managers don't get flustered easily when they face sudden or surprising problems that are even complex many times. They generally tend to keep their calm and immediately get down to finding quick solutions. This comes from the fact that Indians are exposed to all kinds of uncertainties and surprises right from childhood; therefore, sudden problems do not affect their focus. Indian managers tend to be able to handle complex situations easily and thrive in pressure cooker situations.

Arun Maira, a former member of the Planning Commission of India, said, *"The Indian manager's resourcefulness, creativity, and ability to innovate on a shoestring budget are unmatched, and have made them highly sought-after in today's competitive business world."* These three traits, namely resourcefulness, quick-on-the-feet thinking, and cost-consciousness by working with perennially limited resources simultaneously, have made Indian managers *"Jugaadus"* at work.

- Working through complex social hierarchies comes easily for an Indian manager. This is essentially a required skill in an Indian workplace.
- Indians are good at adapting to new environments and changes. It is common in Indian companies to see employees being transferred to different cities in India, say every 3 or 5 years, as part of their career growth plan or business needs. This is a big issue in some other developed countries, but Indians, being generally adaptive, navigate through these changes relatively smoothly.
- This is not unique to Indian managers, but it is essential to mention it here. Indian managers understand the local

culture and business environment, which is necessary for doing business in India.

- Doing business in India is still complex, though we are improving on the "Ease of Doing Business" front. Yet, our laws, regulations and compliance procedures are complicated. Navigating through these complexities is a competency that Indian managers have acquired right from childhood. For example, understanding quickly the import duty structure for products with their myriad slabs and cesses comes easy for Indians while it is not for others. Working through these complexities has made the thinking of Indian managers sharper and more resilient.

- India is diverse by nature, and Indian managers are in a position to relate and work with people of diverse geographies, backgrounds, languages, and cultures. *"Indian managers have a strong sense of empathy and an innate ability to connect with people from different backgrounds, which makes them excellent leaders in today's diverse global workforce,"* said Kiran Mazumdar-Shaw, Chairperson of Biocon and I agree.

- Unlike some Western countries, Indian managers don't take work-life balance seriously. In fact, this is a new and upcoming concept in the lives of Indian professionals. So far, Indians spend time on work beyond working hours and days without expecting any additional compensation. It is widespread for Indians to work even during the weekends if they have to complete a work-related task. In that sense, they are hard working.

- Indian managers come with a blend of technical skills and business acumen, mostly doing Engineering in their graduation and Business Administration in their Masters. BE/B Tech + MBA is a combination that you will find abundant among managers in many Indian large corporates. My first company, Godrej, had a practice of visiting B-Schools to hire Management Trainees every year. By default, it would take only MBAs with an engineering background as it felt that candidates with this background were logical thinkers and good at problem solving. They brought a techno-commercial perspective, which is essential in many business situations. Whenever people from companies abroad visited Godrej, and this point was put across to them, they always felt impressed by this, corroborating with the quality of managers they saw during their meetings in Godrej across businesses, functions, and levels. Not just in Godrej, but you will notice this trend of hiring young managers with engineering and MBA degrees across many Indian corporations like Tatas, Reliance, Infosys, and so on.

- Narayana Murthy of Infosys said of Indian managers: *"Indian managers are highly adept at building strong relationships and networks, which is crucial in a country where personal connections are highly valued."* This is a valid observation, and I agree with it completely. We have seen in the earlier chapters how businesses work on the back of relationships in India.

- One aspect you will notice in India is that Indian managers are usually subservient to their bosses. This is part of the Indian family culture, where following the head of the family without much questioning is very common. The same tradition extends to the workplace as well. One can see some deviation in new-age companies and with the Nextgen youth, but by and large, staff in India are pliant with their superiors, and they seldom go against the grain.

- For more than two centuries, India was under colonial rule. The colonial hangover is yet to leave Indian mindsets even after seventy five years of Independence.

Therefore, Indians at businesses tend to treat people from foreign companies with a lot of respect and regard. Indian business people and managers tend to attach a lot of reverence to the opinions of foreigners, sometimes even negating their fellow citizens' views. This is typical in India. In Japan, the Japanese always give more weight to the opinions of their fellow citizens. The derived implication is that Indians are more open minded to learning from others instead of maintaining rigid ideas. This also brings in the adaptable nature of Indians in general. We tend to adapt and change ourselves to suit the environment quickly, a significant positive trait for success in business. For example, you will notice that even Indians have started handing over their business cards like the Japanese or people from the Far East do, which is to hold the card with both hands. And while doing this, spell your name for the visitor's benefit. Similarly, observing the Japanese addressing everyone with a *San* suffix, Indians also address Japanese with *San* these days. At the same time, when meeting with Americans, they follow the American way of just addressing them by their first names. But within Indian companies, superiors are often addressed with a "Sir" suffix even today!

- Indian managers, particularly those who come from non-metro towns of India, tend to see themselves with an inferiority complex because of their perceived lack of fluent English-speaking skills. This phenomenon is rapidly changing as more and more Indians are getting exposed to English education. So, they tend to keep their opinions to themselves in crucial business negotiations or accept the proposals of their counterparts. Having been on the other side as part of the Japanese delegation and American delegation in my work roles, I have observed that Indians tend to become kind negotiators, particularly with people from other nationalities when the same Indian managers are very aggressive in negotiations with fellow Indians This, I reckon, is due to the colonial hangover and submissive mindset over the generations, which I believe we will get over soon.

- Indian corporations and even SMEs have the practice of adopting a value system as part of their guiding principles. Indian managers are adept at following established value systems even if their personal beliefs contradict these.

- If the Japanese are generalists and Americans are specialists, what are Indians? In my eyes, Indians are "diversified specialists". At the outset, Indians are specialists who revel in a particular subject, function, line, etc. However, given an opportunity to diversify, they pick up the skill sets required and do well. Indian managers are not opposed to job rotation, though given a choice, they would like to stick to their core domain. But, when an opportunity lands, they don't shy away from it and make a success of it. Therefore, I would like to call them "diversified specialists."

- Above all this, if there is one attribute of Indian managers that stands out, it is the "Getting things done" attitude. When sufficiently empowered, Indian managers tend to put in their best efforts, find creative ways to overcome obstacles, show resilience in the face of adversities, and yet complete the task without giving excuses. In this, I would say that Indians go by Machiavelli's principle of *"The end justifies the means."*

Of late, we find that Indian-origin managers are in great demand in America, which, as a society, is most open to welcoming talent. At last count, more than twenty corporations are headed by CEOs of Indian origin now. In a recent article that appeared in the Times of India, Gopalakrishnan (Author and Business commentator who worked with Hindustan Unilever and Tata Group) and Ranjan Banerjee (Dean of BITS School of Management) attributed this *"to the coming together of few factors that created a secret sauce."* These factors were and I quote from the article:

- *"Growing up in a crushingly competitive and highly aspirational environment.*
- *Exposure to extraordinary personal setbacks that accelerate personal learning.*
- *Ability to work hard with intuitive adaptability and creativity.*
- *Ability to think in English."*

Now, I would like to add the skill of managing crises efficiently and calmly to the above four ingredients of the secret sauce that has made Indian managers highly successful in India and on foreign shores. In conclusion, I would say that the making of an Indian manager is due to her inborn survival instincts plus her exposure to competitive environments through education.

Chapter 6

Conclusion

That India is a diverse and complex country is evident to all. This diversity and variation make it a tough market to do business in. Yet, many Indian businesses have demonstrated remarkable success over a sustained period. Just that, to be successful in India, it requires a deep understanding of the business practices and inherent management styles followed by Indian businesses.

After considering all the key aspects of Indian management, is there a simple way to describe or summarise them?

Yes. One acronym that encapsulates the key features of the Indian management style would be "R.O.S.H.I.N.I" where

- R stands for relationships and trust
- O stands for owned by family, managed by professionals
- S stands for skilled in managing chaos
- H stands for heterogeneity and diversification
- I stands for innovation that is frugal and *Jugaad*
- N stands for nurture for the long term
- I stands for instinctive decision making

When you delve into each of the above in detail, Nadar's summation of Indian management in the quote mentioned at the beginning of this chapter makes a lot of sense – That Indian management is not a science but an art. In one of the guest lectures I attended of Rajendra Joshi, Ex-Managing Director, Accenture Technology, he likened the Western way of management or doing business to a Symphony Orchestra. In the Western style of music, players know precisely what they will play in the concert, rehearse together well, and have the notes in front of them for their parts, with a conductor overseeing the group's performance and everyone playing to clockwork precision.

On the other hand, the Indian way of managing is like an Indian Classical Vocal concert. The performers are talented, skilled, and trained. They turn up on stage for a show without much rehearsal, play without notes, etc., but perform instinctively, reacting to each other on stage while delivering a top-notch musical experience. If you have watched a Carnatic concert or a Hindustani music concert, you can relate to what I say. Magic happens on stage, but it is all mostly by instinct and the inherent talent of the musicians. Indian business almost works in the same way – by instinctive leadership and depending more on the individuals than processes.

Therefore, the Indian management method is hardly a science but an art that ultimately works and has been providing results for Indian corporations for a long period now.

It is time for the world to take notice of this emerging Indian style of management, which deftly combines some working aspects of established techniques with its own indigenous features. Understanding this style will go a long way towards helping both Indians and foreigners do business in India more effectively in the future.

"India's Decade" is how global commentators see India's coming of age as a country in terms of its economic performance. Morgan Stanley's Blue paper of October 2022 says, *"India has the conditions in place for an economic boom fuelled by Offshoring, Investment in Manufacturing, the energy transition (from fossil-based to New Energy) and the country's advanced Digital Infrastructure. These drivers will make it the 3rd largest economy and stock market by the end of this decade, we estimate."*

However, Bob Sternfels, CEO of McKenzie & Co., says, *"It will not only be India's decade but India's century[25]! With all key elements in place – a large working population, multinational companies reimagining global supply chains, and a country leapfrogging at digital scale to achieve something not just for the Indian economy but potentially for the world."*

In November 2022, Chetan Ahya, in a piece for *The Financial Times*[26], argued that investors' continuing search for the next big thing would end with India. The author sums it up: *"We estimate that India is set to drive a fifth of global growth in the coming decade. We think this offers a compelling opportunity for multinationals and global investors in a world starved of growth."*

The World Bank, too, in a report titled "Navigating the Storm"[27] released in December 2022, said, *"India is better positioned to navigate global headwinds than other major emerging economies."*

In many years of watching and tracking global commentary on India, I have not seen such a confluence of assessments about the Indian economy's prospects as now. To borrow the famous phrase from Paul Coelho, it seems that "the whole universe is conspiring" to make India succeed.

While it is India's time, and many opportunities abound for the country, it is also essential to recognise that it is a challenging place for those not from India to do business.

In this context, I believe this is the right time to properly understand and portray the Indian style of management and doing business, which is what this book attempts to do. Returning to that question-

and-answer session in our management institute with Gurcharan Das, he also said that one should not wait for someone else to define what the Indian style of management is. That quip stayed with me, and the outcome is this book.

References

Chapter 1 – Introduction

1. Bharat Forge: https://www.ibef.org/download/Bharat_Forge_Limited.pdf

Chapter 2 – Japanese Style of Management

2. *Poka-Yoke*: https://asq.org/
3. *Ishikawa*:https://www.techtarget.com/whatis/definition/fishbone-diagram
4. Share of employees feeling severely stressed at work in Japan 1997-2021https://www.statista.com/statistics/623230/japan-stress-at-work/
5. World IQ levels https://wisevoter.com/country-rankings/average-iq-by-country/
6. *Gembaism:* https://doi.org/10.4337/9781788979757.00022
7. *Ringi* system: https://www.inventurejapan.com/culture/business/ringi

Chapter 3 – American Style of Management

8. Capitalism: https://www.imf.org/external/pubs/ft/fandd/2015/06/basics.htm
9. Lord Maynard Keynes: https://en.wikipedia.org/wiki/John_Maynard_Keynes
10. Top Risk Takers: https://www.olbg.com/blogs/biggest-risk-takers

11. 5 reasons why the US is great on innovation: https://www.usnews.com/opinion/economic-intelligence/articles/2016-01-08/5-reasons-the-us-is-great-for-innovation

Chapter 4A – History of Indian Management

12. Management lessons from *Artha Sasthra*: https://theintactone.com/2019/08/09/mcie-u1-topic-3-management-lessons-from-kautilya-arthashastra/
13. Management lessons from *Vedas*: https://www.vedic-management.com/chanakya-six-principles-of-vedic-management/
14. Evolution of Indian Management: https://www.researchgate.net/publication/339200306_Evolution_of_Indian_Management_Towards_a_New_Paradigm_of_Knowledge_Creation_in_Management_and_Leadership
15. HBR Case Study - The Dabbawala System: https://www.hbs.edu/faculty/Pages/item.aspx?num=38410
16. The Fortune at the bottom of the pyramid: https://www.strategy-business.com/article/11518

Chapter 4B – Diversity in Management Styles in India

17. % of vegetarians in Gujarat: Union Government Sample Registration System Baseline Survey 2014 [large states] + Nutrition Journal [NE States]
18. Why Business Runs In The Gujaratis Blood?: https://taazakhabarnews.com/why-business-runs-in-the-gujaratis-blood/
19. Chettiar community: http://nagaratharbusinessconnections.com/blog/index.php/articles/business-communities-of-india#:~:text=The%20predominant%20business%20communities%20in,Shettys)%2C%20Reddys%20and%20Nadars.

Chapter 5E – Flexible Indians

20. VUCA World: https://en.wikipedia.org/wiki/Volatility,_uncer
tainty,_complexity_and_ambiguity

Chapter 5G – Family-Owned but Professionally Managed

21. Article on Family-owned business becoming professionally managed: https://economictimes.indiatimes.com/et-high-flier/family-business-now-need-to-be-professional/articleshow/7759279.cms?from=mdr

Chapter 5H – Indians and Decision-Making

22. Salesforce Survey on how data was used for decision-making in Indian companies: https://economictimes.indiatimes.com/tech/technology/80-indian-business-leaders-say-data-crucial-in-decision-making-report/articleshow/99845304.cms?from=mdr

Chapter 5I – Indian Businesses and Ethics

23. Survey on Ethics in India: https://www.forbesindia.com/article/leaderboard/for-indian-companies-growth-trumps-ethics/47439/1
24. Indian consumers on Ethics: https://www.expresscomputer.in/news/indian-consumers-willing-to-pay-more-for-ethically-produced-goods-opentext-survey/79819/

Chapter 6 - Conclusion

25. India's decade: https://economictimes.indiatimes.com/news/economy/indicators/its-not-indias-decade-its-indias-century-says-mckinseys-bob-sternfels/articleshow/93937057.cms
26. India growth story: https://www.ft.com/content/489cc92c-c950-47de-ad5f-586b9da33b70

27. Navigating the Storm: https://www.worldbank.org/en/news/press-release/2022/12/05/india-better-positioned-to-navigate-global-headwinds-than-other-major-emerging-economies-new-world-bank-report

Acknowledgements

My tryst with writing started when I started blogging more than a decade ago. The overwhelmingly positive response I received for my posts from family, friends and well-wishers gave me the courage to write on different topics regularly and continue with it till today. Back in 2011, I wrote a blog titled *IIM – Has the time come?* IIM – refers here to the Indian Instincts of Management. In that post, I asked if there is something called the Indian management style. The post got an excellent response by way of readership and reader interaction as well. When Author, Former Diplomat and Member of Parliament Dr Shashi Tharoor retweeted the blog on Twitter (now X), it gave the post plenty of visibility as he has millions of followers. When I thought of writing a book, my first idea was to develop that blog post and expand the topic into a full-fledged book. Therefore, I want to express my profound gratitude to Dr Tharoor for sharing the post, the overwhelming response to which gave me an idea for the book's subject.

Such a book on a serious topic cannot be written without the help of others. I am thankful to my friend Dinesh Jain, a finance Consultant, who helped do a first pass on the portion related to the Marwari business style. Similarly, I thank Paras Shah, Entrepreneur and Tech Enthusiast, for validating my premise on the Gujarati way of doing business and sharing some insights on the topic.

During this book writing journey, I have had rounds of discussions with Sudharshan Srinivasan, a good friend and a Communications and Marketing specialist. As an author himself, Sudharshan acted as an excellent sounding board for ideas for presenting the book, which helped me immensely, for which I am indebted.

My thanks to Bijay Nair, a friend and an author whose tips on publishing the book were handy.

I am eternally thankful to Madhavan Narayanan, senior Editor and Commentator, for his kind efforts in taking the work of a first-time author like me to the publishing community.

I thank my very good friend, philosopher, and guide Gopalakrishnan, a thought leader in his own right for writing the foreword in his own inimitable style for the book.

I am thankful to the team at Notion Press for publishing the book and taking it to readers.

I want to thank all my family members for being pillars of support in my life so far. My gratitude to Uma, Shreya, and my parents - Bhama and Subramania Iyer, for their constant encouragement and for being there with me always.